The Sumerian Civilization

An Enthralling Overview of Sumer and the Ancient Sumerians

Free limited time bonus

Stop for a moment. We have a free bonus set up for you. The problem is this: we forget 90% of everything that we read after 7 days. Crazy fact, right? Here's the solution: we've created a printable, 1-page pdf summary for this book that you're reading now. All you have to do to get your free pdf summary is to go to the following website: **https://livetolearn.lpages.co/enthrallinghistory/**

Once you do, it will be intuitive. Enjoy, and thank you!

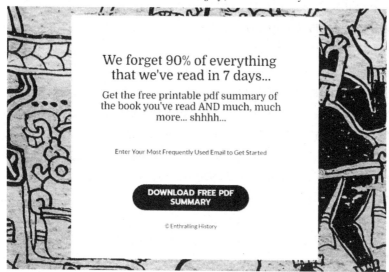

We forget 90% of everything that we've read in 7 days...

Get the free printable pdf summary of the book you've read AND much, much more... shhhh...

Enter Your Most Frequently Used Email to Get Started

DOWNLOAD FREE PDF SUMMARY

© Enthralling History

Contents

Introduction

In most of us lies a tinge of an adventurous spirit. We crave to investigate the mysterious, the aloof, the unknown. Few of us will ever have the chance to physically follow through on those thoughts. Luckily for us, the busy, technology-driven, and commercialized lives that we are caught up in also provide us with the means to satisfy that conscious or subconscious craving.

Through books and film, we can satisfy our curiosity and enrich our minds. History, as a whole, and ancient history, in particular, is often more mysterious and awe-inspiring than fiction. The higher goal of learning about history, though, is that it should ultimately teach us not to repeat humanity's past mistakes.

Modern ways of cooperation between many different fields of science have clarified much ancient historical data, most of which is relevant today. For example, climate change is a pressing issue today. Palaeobotanists, archaeologists, and other researchers have discovered that our ancient forbearers, without industrialization and large-scale pollution, dealt with climate change on several occasions and thrived again afterward.

With this book, we would like to draw you into the surprisingly sophisticated world of the ancient Sumerians. Reckoned for centuries to be the first people to develop civilization, they flourished at the dawn of history between the Euphrates and Tigris Rivers. They lived, made merry, were sad, and were afraid. They learned, worked, worshiped, fought, and made peace. They invented practical solutions and tools, developed ideas and explanations, and manufactured products from raw materials without external aid or prior knowledge.

The Sumerians invented a list of around thirty-nine "firsts" literally from nothing over a relatively brief period. They solved the challenges of their society through innovation when the need arose. We should not only be in awe of their abilities but also of the fact that we still use some of their innovations, albeit modernized, to this day.

Ancient civilizations sprouted in fertile river valleys on every continent. The most well-known of these is probably the ancient Egyptian civilization of the Nile Valley. Some of these civilizations declined, disappeared, and were forgotten as time passed until their ruins and artifacts were rediscovered by chance—like the Sumerians. In other instances, the deciphering of ancient texts set scholars on the trail of discovery—again, like the Sumerians!

The exact timelines for Sumerian settlements and the development of innovative solutions to ease their lives are not known for sure. The styles and sophistication in the manufacture of pottery are often used to determine timelines and changes in culture during prehistory throughout the ancient Near East. The Sumerian civilization's timeline is based on information gathered from multiple sites.

Carbon-14 dating and other modern scientific dating methods have confirmed some periods. There is little consensus amongst scholars about the exact timeline of events, inventions, and lengths of reigns. Thus, exact chronologies have not been set up and remain a cause of disagreement. We have endeavored to stick to a consistent timeline, but it is important to note that this timeline might not exactly agree with other sources you have read before this. The lack of an exact timeline is part of the Sumerians' intrigue and provides food for speculation, theories, serious history fans, and even ufologists.

In the 19th century, attentive Assyriologists were on the trail of a well-known ancient civilization, the Assyrians. As they investigated the Assyrian culture, they noticed a different culture and legacy. And thus, the magnificent world of the ancient Sumerian civilization was revealed. Biblical scholars and archaeologists jumped at the chance to excavate the land of the biblical and Koranic patriarch Abraham's birth. By this time, they already knew that the Chaldeans of the Bible were later inhabitants of that land.

We still do not know enough about the Sumerians, especially if we consider that their civilization waxed and waned for roughly four thousand years. The bulk of our knowledge stems from archaeological excavations and deciphered clay tablets from the ancient library of King Ashurbanipal of Assyria in Nineveh. More than thirty thousand cuneiform clay tablets were discovered here and elsewhere, and many are still undeciphered. The Assyrian cuneiform tablets were in several languages and styles, and amongst them were lexicons, which set scholars on the path to identify the languages and start deciphering them.

When the Sumerian people, who called themselves the "black-headed people," arrived in the land that would later become Sumer in southern Mesopotamia, there were other groups of nomadic and semi-nomadic people living between the Tigris and Euphrates Rivers and throughout the ancient Near East. Where they came from still baffles scholars. Their genealogy has still not been unraveled despite more than 140 years of excavations and linguistic analysis by many scholars and Sumerologists.

Because the Sumerians invented writing and later recorded the history, myths, and beliefs of earlier generations from oral transmissions, we have their own interpretations and explanations.

What did they believe? How did they explain human existence and the purpose of life? How did they explain natural phenomena?

Hypotheses about the origins of the Sumerians vary greatly, and theories and conclusions cover many geographical possibilities. They might have come from the Levant, Anatolia, the Zagros Mountains, ancient East Asia, the Indus Valley, or somewhere in the Indian Ocean. Genetic analysis of ancient Mesopotamian skeletons that compare DNA with modern Marsh Arabs from southern Iraq confirmed that they are closely related. Skeletons from the excavations at Ur by the late Leonard Wooley were recently discovered in still-unpacked crates after nearly a century. One can only hope that DNA from this may finally identify the Sumerians' origins to a reasonably certain degree.

Chapter 1 – The Ubaid Period

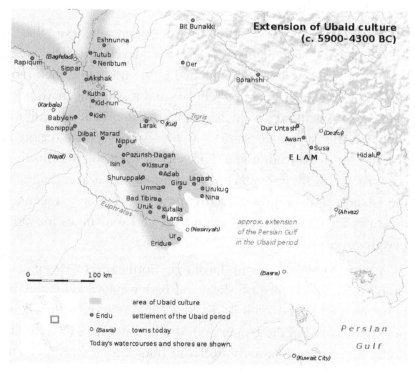

Map showing sites of the Ubaid culture.
Map Ubaid culture-en.svg: NordNordWestderivative work: Rowanwindwhistler, CC BY-SA 4.0 https://creativecommons.org/licenses/by-sa/4.0 via Wikimedia Commons; https://commons.wikimedia.org/wiki/File:Map_Ubaid_culture-es.svg

How It Began

There is no universally accepted timeline for settlements in ancient Mesopotamia, but it is agreed by scholars that semi-nomadic hunter-gatherers had been settling in Mesopotamia from around 10,000 to 8000 BCE. There are signs of cultivated date palms even before 10,000 BCE in the south, where Sumer would later be founded. The exact origins of these prehistoric people groups and the subsequent development of the Ubaid culture are so interwoven with the rest of the ancient Near East that scholars agreed at a workshop in 2006 that it developed from a mixed heritage diffused peaceably through inter-relationships. The first settlements were made up of nomadic and semi-nomadic groups who started agricultural activities at seasonal settlements.

Mainstream archaeologists and historians believe that the Mesopotamian settlements, which later developed into villages, cities, and civilizations, first happened in the north and then moved south. Other equally qualified scholars and researchers have posited that the Ubaid culture, as the forerunner of the Sumerian culture of southern Mesopotamia, started in the Arabian Gulf region and spread northward from there. This spread from south to north and outward seems the most logical conclusion. What is certain is that the Ubaid culture is present across the entire Fertile Crescent, and timelines are continuously pushed back and sometimes forward by new discoveries.

At the Neolithic site of Jarmo in northeastern Mesopotamia (Iraq), there is evidence of wheat and barley cultivation dating back to between 8000 and 7000 BCE. New cultures and the invention of pottery occurred in the Upper and Middle Euphrates areas at Halaf (today in Syria) and Samarra (today in Iraq) during this time. These semi-nomads also brought domesticated animals like sheep, goats, cattle, and pigs with them as they moved southward. It is believed that some came from the Zagros Mountains region, where animal domestication started earlier.

Identification of Settlement Areas

The first distinctive sedentary period in the land of Sumer is known as the Ubaid period after Tell al-'Ubaid. This substantial tell was discovered four miles (six kilometers) north of the large ancient city of Uruk.

Semi-nomadic tribes of Semitic and other people groups were already settled in some of the areas when the Sumerians or "black-headed people" arrived in southern Mesopotamia. These people called themselves "black-headed people" in later texts after they invented a writing system—the first that we know of in the world.

At some point, the settlers started making clay vessels for domestic use, such as plates, bowls, and containers for food storage. These clay vessels were either lightly or thoroughly fired and in a buff or greenish color. They were decorated with black, brown, or purple geometric lines. This is known as Hassuna-style pottery after the site where it was first discovered in northern Mesopotamia.

Between 6500 and 5000 BCE, settlements continued to spread. By around 6000 BCE, there were signs of sedentary farming communities that relied on irrigation rather than rainfall for crop cultivation in the more arid south of Mesopotamia toward the Persian Gulf. The people farmed the land, kept domesticated animals, and fished from the rivers and the sea. Some archaeologists posit that these lifestyles represent three different ethnic groups: those that cultivated crops, those that practiced animal husbandry, and those that fished the marshes.

The material culture of the Ubaid period across most of the Fertile Crescent varies in duration. In southern Mesopotamia, the Ubaid culture is dated from approximately 6500 BCE to 3800 BCE (or 4000 BCE by some) and as late as c. 5300 BCE to 3900 BCE by others. Due to the lengthy Ubaid period, archaeologists have divided it into six stages, from Ubaid 0 to Ubaid 5.

The dating and spread of Ubaid influences across the Levant are primarily identified through pottery styles, similar cultural evidence, and related periods in time. As already mentioned, scholars are not in agreement on whether the Ubaid culture spread from northern Mesopotamia to the south or from south to north.

The oldest Ubaid settlement in southern Mesopotamia so far discovered is a small tell close to Larsa called Tell el-'Oueili, which dates from 6500 BCE to 5400 BCE. It was discovered by André Parrot and excavated between 1976 and 1989 by the French archaeologist Jean-Louis Huot.

This discovery pushed back the timeline of the Ubaid period and necessitated the adding of Ubaid 0 to the already set Ubaid 1 to Ubaid 5 chronology. Most of the oldest Mesopotamian Ubaid sites are located in the south, where other groups had already settled. To date, there is no consensus among scholars regarding the origins of the people, the settlement dates, and how or why the earliest sedentary cultures flourished in the alluvial plains of the more arid south.

The area is poor in natural resources like minerals and timber, and the flooding of the rivers is unpredictable and untimely for crops, necessitating irrigation. And yet, it may be these difficult circumstances that drove the development of excellent and awe-inspiring innovations. The inhabitants used what was available, cleverly innovated technology when needed, and even made sickles from hard-baked clay for harvesting. The fauna and flora indicate that farmers at this earliest Ubaid site of Tell el-'Oueili used draft animals (oxen) and relied on crops like barley, which could tolerate the alluvial silt's salinity.

The following Ubaid periods are typical of a developing society, with every new style leading to the next. Naturally, the egalitarian society adapted since the people needed a group of people with organizational skills and oversight for communal projects, such as canal-building and maintenance. This, in turn, led to societal differentiation and eventually class structures and labor divisions.

Houses were built from mudbricks and straw or reeds. Tripartite dwellings were generally built around a larger centrally situated multi-roomed house, which then formed a central village around which smaller villages developed. It is possible that the main village would then become the leading force, with the sub-villages being subordinate to it in decision-making and labor distribution.

One can imagine how much labor would have been needed for the maintenance of canals, which would have been plagued by regular silting-up from the flooding rivers. Innovations during this phase did not only ease labor-intensive agricultural activities. Canoes and nets for the fishers of the marshes were also improved.

Organized settlements led to the building of communal centers, with an emphasis on religious buildings. Religious centers became the village centers, with each village having its own patron deity. Like the houses, these buildings were constructed of mudbricks and reeds or straw covered with clay.

The Origins of Eridu

For a long time, researchers, historians, and archaeologists believed that the first city in Sumer was Eridu. This assumption appeared to be confirmed by ancient Sumerian texts describing Sumerian beliefs about the beginning of the world. The Sumerians believed that the deities chose the oldest city when they decided to bring kingship down to Earth. The chief deity, Enki, was said to have built his temple in Eridu. It was only later, with more modern dating methods, that it was discovered that the city of Uruk predates Eridu. Nevertheless, the archaeological site of Eridu provides us with the best-illustrated cultural development record of the period.

Eridu was one of five cities that predated the Great Flood of Sumerian myths. Interestingly, this Great Flood myth is remarkably similar to the biblical Great Flood as described in Genesis. A renowned Sumerologist, Thorkild Jacobsen, named the Sumerian creation myth the *Eridu Genesis*. Excavations in Sumer at the ancient city of Ur confirmed that there was a very thick layer of mud with signs of habitation underneath from the time before the flood.

The city of Eridu was located on the Arabian Gulf and was the southernmost city of Sumer. The earliest settlement phase of the Eridu site is dated to around 5400 BCE. The main tell has eight layers. Eridu's ziggurat was rebuilt seventeen times, each time larger and more elaborate until it represented the common style of later temples. This common style is a tripartite building on a platform consisting of a long rectangular room with rooms leading off the long sides. The central room had an altar, and there was a niche in the wall for a statue of the local patron deity; in Eridu's case, it would have been Enki.

The original Eridu village developed into a town and then into a city with surrounding villages during and following the Ubaid period, despite the salinity-prone soil, which limited its agricultural prowess. In later periods when the city became uninhabitable, it was still used as a cult center until almost the end of the 1st millennium BCE. The city was abandoned and taken over by sandy dunes and silt, but the ziggurat was still functional. Building remnants on a small site nearby suggest that the priests who looked after the temple may have lived there.

During the Eridu phase of the Ubaid period, another ethnic group with its own distinctive culture from a different southern settlement became part of Eridu's population. The second period of Eridu culture is called the Hadji Muhammed phase after this group, and it dates from c. 4800 to 4500 BCE. The Ubaid 2 phase saw extensive growth in settlements and agriculture.

Major canals and irrigation channels with levees and sluice gates drove increased food production, which could support larger communities and enabled the storage of surplus crops. The population growth meant that attention could be channeled into other occupations. Through trading, the Sumerians could supplement their lack of natural resources and raw materials, which included certain minerals, obsidian, and timber. This, in turn, led to further innovations. For example, plows were later fitted with metal cutting edges obtained through trade.

A centralized organization and administration were a natural outcome of these developments. Social levels were undoubtedly impacted, and class stratification took over. It is surmised by some scholars that the heads of extended families may have become local chieftains. These positions were sometimes hereditary. In the beginning, the chieftains would have mainly functioned as advisors, managed inter-community squabbles, and functioned as judges in their communities.

It needs to be mentioned that earlier farmers made use of extended family structures to cope with labor-intensive agricultural activities. During the Ubaid period, labor from outside the family became necessary due to increased production and specialization in other occupations, such as the manufacturing of tools and pottery.

Distinctive Styles of Pottery Discovered by Archaeologists

The distinctive Ubaid pottery, after which this period is named and which, in turn, received its name from the site where it was first identified, was meticulously crafted from light-colored clay. It was sometimes only lightly fired. Sometimes, pottery was thoroughly baked in kilns. Traces of such kilns were found at Tell al-'Ubaid.

The clay dried to a neutral buff or gentle greenish hue and was decorated with black, brown, or purple paint. The painted decorations are in the form of lines, geometric shapes, floral patterns, and animal shapes.

Painted shallow dish decorated with geometric designs in dark paint. From Tell al-'Ubaid, Late Ubaid period, c. 5200–4200 BCE.
Zunkir, CC BY-SA 4.0 https://creativecommons.org/licenses/by-sa/4.0 via Wikimedia Commons; https://commons.wikimedia.org/wiki/File:Shallow_dish_-_Ubaid.jpg

Grave goods recovered from Tell al-'Ubaid contained plates, bowls, small kraters (also spelled craters; these were open vase-shaped vessels with handles), clay tokens, and more. Handles and spouts were added later to the larger kraters. The decorations are less elaborate than the earlier Halaf-style pottery of northern Mesopotamia but similar in style and execution. The paint of the decorations was often applied by the blade-cut method.

Apart from the practical clay wares, there were also ornaments and figurines made of clay. These were in the shapes of animals and humans—men and women—with strangely shaped lizard-like faces.

Overall, the Ubaid period brought forth population growth and progress in every sphere of life. The ever-larger villages spread out, with smaller village settlements on the outskirts and in surrounding areas. Domestic dwellings were built from reeds and clay and then progressed to clay-covered reeds to mudbrick dwellings in the distinct tripartite style. This style was repeated for communal and religious buildings, such as the distinctive ziggurats.

Chapter 2 – The Uruk Period

Sumerian civilization officially started in the Uruk period. This period was characterized by rapid development and numerous cultural and political changes. Settlements had been replaced by villages, which developed, in some cases, into towns. In the Uruk period, it is believed the first cities in the world appeared.

The Uruk period can be divided into two distinct phases. The Early Uruk period dates from c. 4000 to 3500 BCE, and the Late Uruk period dates from c. 3500 to 3000 BCE.

The Sumerians probably arrived during the Ubaid period and took over the already developed villages. The Sumerians developed them into multi-faceted settlements that consisted of hamlets, towns, urban centers, and even cities.

The eastern arm of the Fertile Crescent ends in southern Mesopotamia (modern-day Iraq). As mentioned before, the origins of the Sumerians are not known. All we know for certain is that their language has no connection to any known language group, and their DNA is similar to the modern-day people living in the marshlands in southern Iraq. They called their new country Sumer (*Kengir* in Sumerian), meaning "country of the noble lords."

The Sumerians are thought to be among the most intelligent and innovative peoples of the ancient world because of their numerous inventions and problem-solving skills. According to dictionaries, the historical concept of a civilization is a society characterized by well-developed urban centers, agricultural success, a written language, a central or state government, developed and applied technologies, a common ideology, and shared culture. The Sumerians tick all the boxes; therefore, they are recognized as the first civilization in history.

After settling in southern Mesopotamia, the innovative Sumerians soon invented or modified the plow, which was followed by the invention of the seeder plow. This later plow could distribute the seeds evenly over the plowed soil. A draft animal could also pull it. Later in Sumerian history, after the invention of writing, they produced the first crop cultivation manual, with instructions in the format of a letter from a father to his son. It covered the entire crop cycle—the how and when of every step to be taken from planning to harvesting. It included tips on what to beware of, tasks that should be done, what should not be done, and how to oversee and instruct a laborer.

During the Early Uruk period, the Sumerians followed in the footsteps of their predecessors when it came to architecture. They used the existing tripartite dwellings in which they resided with their extended families. These houses were grouped in proximity to each other and would form a hamlet over time. Small towns were formed as the hamlets started to expand and meet each other, and a new social structure emerged.

Archaeological excavations indicate that Uruk developed from two separate settlements named Eanna and Kullaba, which grew in size and merged to form the first city (Uruk). Further excavations at this site showed that the city was surrounded by walls that were 5.9 miles (9.5 kilometers) long and enclosed an area of 450 hectares

(1,111 acres). It is estimated that the population at this time was around fifty thousand people.

Uruk was considered the most prominent of the Mesopotamian cities for a thousand years. Archaeological evidence and texts confirm that Uruk exercised a certain amount of control over the smaller surrounding villages and towns when it came to trade and political power. However, it is unclear how Uruk's power was enforced, as the administration of the region was decentralized and managed by each of the smaller cities.

What Distinguished Uruk from the Other Cities?

Scholars and historians often ask why Uruk was such a dominant city-state when the city-state of Ur was geographically better located for economic power through trade. Ur was located on a channel of the Euphrates River and lay farther south than Uruk. It was closer to the Persian Gulf—a gateway to the possibly lucrative Arabian and Mediterranean markets. There is no consensus regarding this issue as of yet.

The Late Uruk Period

As the headwaters of the Persian Gulf receded south during the dry spell of the Late Uruk period, the marshlands shrank. Irrigation of the agricultural fields had to be increased. The rivers that used to provide a natural source for irrigation began to shrink due to severe droughts in the north, making it increasingly difficult to feed the growing population. To solve this problem, the Sumerians looked to colonize surrounding and even far-away areas, which was yet another first in history.

Colonization of the neighboring city-states, especially in the Susiana Plain, occurred between 3700 and 3400 BCE. Archaeological evidence of the cultural, artifactual, architectural, and symbolic remains confirm this timeline and location.

Throughout the colonization period, smaller settlements like Tell Brak and Hamoukar in the north of Mesopotamia were colonized by Uruk. Hamoukar was established to the north of Uruk during the Early Uruk period. These city-states were originally part of the extensive trade routes for bitumen and copper.

It is interesting to note that the expansion and colonized areas were not managed from Uruk but were instead run locally through regional administrative centers. These administrative centers were able to control the manufacture and trade of objects. Cylinder seals, pottery, and other materials excavated in these regions confirm that trading colonies in Syria, Anatolia, and Iran shared the same administrative systems and pottery styles at this time. The products from each center were manufactured locally.

The White Temple of Uruk

Visible from a distance, this magnificent ziggurat, known as the Anu Ziggurat, had a magnificent white temple dedicated to the sky god Anu at its top, which would have dominated the skyline. Located in modern-day Warka, Iraq, archaeologists estimate that it would have taken 1,500 laborers around 5 years to complete its construction. These laborers would have had to work ten-hour days. It is surmised that some laborers would have been coerced or forced to do the work and that only some of their labor was paid for.

Remains of the ziggurat at Uruk that had the White Temple.
tobeytravels, CC BY-SA 2.0 https://creativecommons.org/licenses/by-sa/2.0 via Wikimedia Commons; https://commons.wikimedia.org/wiki/File:White_Temple_ziggurat_in_Uruk.jpg

The White Temple of Uruk is a typical example of a "high temple." It emerged in this region to honor the patron deity of a city. This rectangular temple was built in the tripartite style, with the corners oriented to the four cardinal directions: north, south, east, and west. This exceptional whitewashed temple, measuring 57.4 feet by 76.4 feet (17.5 by 23.3 meters), would have been a spectacular sight under the midday sun.

As was typical in tripartite buildings, a long central hall was flanked by smaller rooms. An altar was located at the end of the hall, and a niche in a prominent wall for a statue of the patron god would have had a place of pride.

Hamoukar

The settlement of this city dates back to the 5th millennium BCE and was inhabited during the Ubaid and Early Uruk periods. The excavated city is in northeastern Syria, near the Iraq and Turkey borders.

Obsidian processing was the main commercial activity at this settlement. This shows us the people's innovation and drive to ensure sustainable living. The raw obsidian was not locally available and had to be imported from southern Anatolia, which was around 70 miles (112.65 kilometers) away. The manufactured obsidian tools and weapons were then exported to southern Mesopotamia, resulting in the generation of income for the inhabitants. The obsidian workshops covered an area of around 692 acres (280 hectares), and chemical analysis of the obsidian found here confirmed that it came from the foothills of Mount Nemrut in modern-day Turkey.

In Hamoukar, evidence shows the emergence of class structures, with the elites accumulating wealth. They bought their food and other supplies from surrounding villages.

After Hamoukar became an established and wealthy city, the inhabitants realized that the city needed more security. They built a wall around it, thus establishing the first walled city of which we are aware. The urbanization process here can be attributed to economic growth rather than people being coerced or forced to live there as laborers.

At its peak, Hamoukar had around 20,000 inhabitants and covered an area of 259 acres (105 hectares). Hamoukar did not only export tools and weapons to the south. New evidence confirms that they also traded with the north. This northern trade was independently undertaken, proving that Hamoukar had its own rulers or at least some form of independence.

Before the battle of Hamoukar, the inhabitants had progressed to manufacturing copper tools and weapons, making it a target for conquerors due to the city's wealth and accomplishments.

Battle of Hamoukar

The battle of Hamoukar is referred to as the first incident of urban warfare. Excavations have indicated that the attack on the city must have been well-planned. It appears as though it took place rather suddenly, though, catching the inhabitants off-guard. Their unpreparedness might be partly due to the surrounding ten-foot (three-meter) thick walls, which likely left them feeling secure. The invaders somehow set fire to the city. Walls and roofs of buildings that were not consumed by the fire collapsed. Archaeologists have uncovered enough artifacts from the rubble to form a good idea of how the city was destroyed.

Fairly recent excavations have uncovered over 2,300 egg-shaped clay sling bullets from two of the collapsed administrative buildings. Further evidence of the battle, such as twelve graves of male victims, was also found underneath the rubble. Archaeologists are confident the fire that destroyed the city was set by an enemy and was not caused by an earthquake or an accident.

Tell Brak

Tell Brak is located in northeastern Syria. It sits on one of the major ancient trade routes connecting Mesopotamia, Anatolia, Euphrates cities, and Mediterranean seaports. This is one of the largest tells in the area that has been excavated to date.

Tell Brak covered an extensive area of 98 acres (40 hectares) and rose to 131 feet (40 meters) before the excavations. During this city-state's peak, it was spread over an area of between 271 and 395 acres (110 and 160 hectares) and had a population of between 17,000 and 24,000.

Suburbs at Tell Brak

The tell was surrounded by smaller hamlets or suburbs where many of its inhabitants lived. These suburbs cover an area of over 741 acres (300 hectares). Archaeological evidence indicates that this area had been inhabited since the Ubaid period and lasted until the middle of the 1st millennium CE.

Excavations at Tell Brak, Hamoukar, and Tepe Gawra provide archaeologists with pottery and architectural evidence that confirms these city-states shared the same religious, administrative, and social behaviors.

An enormous building for non-residential purposes has been excavated at Tell Brak, exposing walls made from red mudbrick. This majestic building has an entrance with a basalt gateway that has towers on each side. The walls are 6 feet thick (1.85 meters) and 5 feet high (1.5 meters) and are still visible today.

Tel Brak Industry

A craft workshop was excavated in which flint manufacturing, basalt grinding, and mollusk shell inlays took place. Another building for the manufacture of ceramic bowls has been identified, and its purpose was confirmed by the substantial number of mass-produced bowls it contained. A unique chalice made from obsidian and white marble held together with bitumen was also found in this building. This same building even housed an ample collection of stamp seals and sling bullets.

Social Gatherings

The Tell Brak feast hall contained a large number of mass-produced plates and tasseled pots. This building has been identified as a feast hall due to the large ovens with animal remains found in the northern courtyard. The interior of the feast hall contains several large hearths, which would have provided heat during communal gatherings and feasts.

Beer made from barley and groats was apparently consumed at these feasts, and copious amounts of meat were devoured. It would appear that the ancient civilization had a work life, a social life, and a religious life.

Religion

Religious practices were centered on the worship of an all-seeing deity, and a temple in Tell Brak was dedicated to this god, which was the city's patron deity. This temple may indicate that Tell Brak was one of the first cities in northern Mesopotamia that practiced an organized religion—at least as far as we know.

The inhabitants of Tell Brak made votive figurines and symbols that they used to worship their all-seeing god. However, it is possible they worshiped a goddess instead. Scholars surmise that the Sumerian goddess Inanna, who is associated with political power, war, justice, beer, love, and beauty, was the goddess the people of Tell Brak worshiped.

Eye figurines and symbols found at the temple in Tell Brak.
https://commons.wikimedia.org/wiki/File:Augenidole_Syrien_Slg_Ebn%C3%B6ther.jpg

Chapter 3 – The Early Dynastic Period

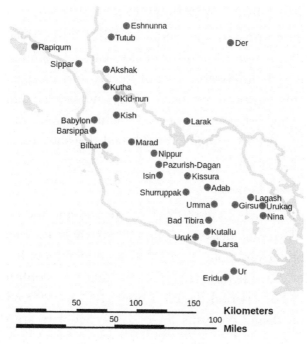

Map of city-states in ancient Sumer.
Ciudades_de_Sumeria.svg: Cratesderivative work: Phirosiberia, CC BY 3.0
https://creativecommons.org/licenses/by/3.0 via Wikimedia Commons;
https://commons.wikimedia.org/wiki/File:Cities_of_Sumer_(en).svg

The Rise of the Early Dynastic Period

Although there are no clearly demarcated eras in the development of Sumer during the Early Dynastic period, scholars have divided it into three phases: Early Dynastic I (c. 2900–2800 BCE), Early Dynastic II (c. 2800–2600 BCE), and Early Dynastic III (c. 2600–2334 BCE). The entire ED (Early Dynastic) period was one of growth and innovations. Many of the "firsts" credited to the Sumerians date to this period and the short bridging phase immediately before it.

Knowledge of this period is largely due to archaeological excavations, later historical records, and deciphering Sumerian writings that date to the later part of the Early Dynastic period. Historians often have to compare several of these sources to come to reasonably reliable conclusions since some of the information, especially from ancient records, is only partly factual.

A good example is the Sumerian King List, which provides valuable information for a discerning researcher, although they are interwoven with impossibly lengthy reigns and lifespans of kings coupled with obviously mythical deeds and beings. Although the Sumerian king list contains several Semitic names of kings and places, it has been reasonably established that the Sumerians were non-Semitic in origin.

Jemdet Nasr Period

During the final phase of the Uruk period and the beginning of the Early Dynastic period, around 3000 BCE to 2900 BCE, a relatively brief overlapping period has been identified. It was named the Jemdet Nasr period after the site that was confirmed to be Sumerian. This period lasted from 3100 to 2900 BCE, and radiocarbon dating confirms these dates. Scholars are divided in their acceptance of the Jemdet Nasr period as a separate phase due to wide cultural similarities with the preceding and following periods.

The scientific world was first alerted to the Jemdet Nasr culture when clay tablets with a proto-cuneiform (Archaic) type of writing were discovered. These tablets had appeared in antiquities markets since around 1903. The writing had already been identified as the Sumerian language due to the discovery of later tablets. An Assyriologist, Stephen Langdon, started excavations at Jemdet Nasr in 1926. The same cultural aspects that were identified at this site were later discovered at many other archaeological sites across southern and central Mesopotamia.

Administrative clay tablet from the Jemdet Nasr Period, Uruk III.
Metropolitan Museum of Art, CC0, via Wikimedia Commons;
https://commons.wikimedia.org/wiki/File:Met_(2)_-
_Administrative_tablet,_Jamdat_Nasr,_Uruk_III_style_-
_3100%E2%80%932900_B.C_(d%C3%A9tail).jpg

The period seems to be an extension of the Uruk period, as it saw the further development of several inventions and characteristics already evident in the Uruk period. Ceramics are present in polychrome and in the distinct monochrome, which were similar to the Ubaid period. The original pictographic writing invented during the Uruk period had developed into a more abstract style by this time. The distinctive wedge shape of cuneiform writing also dates to this Early Dynastic bridging period.

Early Dynastic Period

The Early Dynastic period started at different times across Sumer, at least according to the archaeological record of the sites so far excavated. The one thing that the beginning of Sumerian history to almost the late Early Dynastic period has in common is the insecurity of the chronology and the dates on which they are hung. More radiocarbon dating and modern scientific methods of dating are sorely needed to enable scholars to refine and correlate these dates.

According to early excavations done in the previous century, there appeared to be a break in cultural deposits and established networks around 2900 BCE. At the time, this was explained by the story of the Great Flood. Legends of a universal flood are recorded in the tales of several ANE (ancient Near East) scripts, as well as the biblical flood. Great and widespread floods from circa 2900 to 2800 BCE seemed to be confirmed by very thick mud deposits (11 feet or 3.35 meters). These deposits were found by Leonard Woolley in his excavations at Ur and at other sites by different archaeologists.

The controversy surrounding the reality of such a flood added to the many arguments involving the Sumerian civilization. The problem with the flood story is that the dates, depths of mud layers, and sites where mud layers are present do not correlate. Furthermore, this mud layer does not appear at all the sites that have been excavated.

The delta area of southern Mesopotamia was prone to seasonal floods, especially by the Euphrates River, which caused the rivers to often change course. Even though the Euphrates was relatively shallow, it was known to have wiped away everything in its path on occasion. The various mud layers are better explained as being the results of different floods at different times. These floods would have varied in intensity. The stories of these floods were then passed down orally and combined with myths and legends before eventually being written down.

Cultural Advancements

The First Dynasty of Egypt has been radiocarbon dated to 3100 BCE and is considered by historians to be the oldest dynasty in the world. The Sumerian Early Dynastic period is the first era in Mesopotamia in which a dynastic ruling line can be traced. At the same time, the earliest settlements and villages started to have leadership. It is widely accepted that this role eventually progressed via a line of kinship, with a family head becoming a chieftain and passing leadership on to members of the same family.

Writing progressed from simple pictographic commercial records and transactions. This was due to the development of syllabic representations, which could be more flexibly used. During the Early Dynastic II and III, the first contemporary extant text that can be described as historical is in praise of Enmebaragesi, King of Kish. However, this wasn't erected by just any person; Enmebaragesi commissioned it himself! It is dated to c. 2600 BCE and is housed in the Iraq Museum in Baghdad.

Religion in Ancient Sumer

Similar to previous Sumerian periods, religion played a large role, and the belief that humans were on Earth to serve the gods was firmly entrenched in every aspect of life. Placating and honoring the deities was paramount in the life of every Sumerian. Interestingly, the first gift dedicated by a king to a god that we have definitive proof of was not dedicated to the patron god of the city or that king! The inscription, which was discovered at Tell al-'Ubaid, was from a king of Ur and dedicated to one of the major Sumerian goddesses who influenced daily life. It stated, "Aanepada King of Ur, son of Mesanepada King of Ur, has built this for his lady Ninhursag."

The priests of local deities played an important role. They advised the people at all levels of society. Since they acted as mouthpieces of the deities, they made the will of the gods clear to the people in all matters, whether it was personal or work-related. The priests had to clarify the reasons for a bad experience or situation, such as a calamity or the infertility of people and/or their livestock. The priests were also the interpreters of what the deities needed to right the matter.

They used several methods of divination; reading the entrails of a sheep or goat is a popular example. They also interpreted the dreams and visions of people in their communities. They received direction from the deities via oracles, dreams, and cosmic signs. The priest-kings and later the kings received, acted upon, and communicated the will of the gods to the people.

Priests were also doctors. Due to their association with the deities, they were believed to have the knowledge to define the cause and prescribe a cure, which would all be communicated to them by the gods.

The ziggurats, which were often in the centers of cities, were not built as places of worship. They did not have space for gatherings, despite their monumental size. They were built as a dwelling for the local patron deity, and in larger cities, there might be more than one ziggurat since the people had to honor the supreme deities as well. Large quantities of votive offerings and statuettes and later cuneiform messages on pieces of clay, stone, or other suitable materials were discovered under floors and inside the walls of these buildings and the temples on their tops. These were presumably placed there by priests on behalf of individuals who wanted to plead, implore, or thank a deity.

A wall plaque depicting libations to a seated god; Ur, 2500 BCE.

Structure of Society

The early Sumerians were not class conscious, and it appears that all citizens were equal. This is confirmed by grave goods from cemeteries that were excavated at several archaeological sites, as well as later texts about the early periods. This changed over time, and class structures developed naturally. Changes in individual responsibilities and communal duties, the implementation of leadership and authority, and an accumulation of wealth created stratification among the people.

Increased agricultural production led to the division of labor and specialization of crafts. This was firmly entrenched by the Early Dynastic period. Four main levels of society can be distinguished. These were the priests, the upper class, the lower class, and the slaves. Archaeologists were able to confirm these distinctions from grave goods interred with the dead.

It appears from the artworks of the ED period that the priests and sometimes kings shaved their heads. Women wore their long hair in braids or elaborate coifs piled on their heads. Men had long hair, which was often tied up in a knot. People dressed in skirts or dresses with scalloped hems that overlapped in layers, slightly reminiscent of the feathers of a bird. Jewelry was worn by both men and women, rich and poor, with clear class distinctions obvious in the materials from which it was made. The upper class and rulers wore exquisite adornments made from gold and other precious materials. This has been confirmed by excavations of grave goods with which they were buried.

Men and women had equal rights during this period, and women participated in all parts of society. Kingship was mostly bestowed on males, but we know of one woman, Ku Bau, an innkeeper or brewer of beer, who received the kingship of Kish.

Rise of the Kings, Cities, and City-States

In the early Mesopotamian towns, the first rulers were priests, but they became kings once villages had progressed and enlarged into urban centers. Kingship became an integral part of the social organization, and by the Early Dynastic I period, the priests, the military, and the entire community were lower in status than the local kings. Kings were more secular in function, but their primary objective of pleasing the city's patron god and the major gods of the Sumerian pantheon remained the same. It should be noted that for the Sumerians, the kingship was divine—a gift bestowed by the gods on an elected subject that could be removed if the gods so wished.

The king claimed his appointment to the throne by the city's deity and was seen as representing that deity. The kings portrayed themselves as subservient to the deity's wishes and acted as part of the community in their service to the gods. In artworks, the kings can be seen participating in communal activities like the building of a temple. But at the same time, the portrayals of kings in personalized and named capacities indicate the growth in the status of those leaders. The grave goods from the royal cemetery at Ur and the building of palaces verify this trend.

Votive Relief of Ur-Nanshe, King of Lagash, as the bird god Anzu.
https://commons.wikimedia.org/wiki/File:Relief_Im-dugud_Louvre_AO2783.jpg

The first historically verifiable dynastic king, Mesannepada (Mesanepada), is thought to have started the First Dynasty of Ur around 2670 BCE.

Names of kings often come from inscriptions. Ur-Nanshe, the first king of the First Dynasty of Lagash, added to an inscription about how he honored the goddess Nanshe by building a canal. "For Nanshe he dug the Ninadua-canal, her beloved canal, and extended its far end to the sea."

A votive statuette of a musician named Ur-Nanshe was found in the ruins of a temple at the distant site of Mari in Syria around this same period (c. 2520 BCE). An inscription of his name ran across the shoulders. The superbly carved statuette could have been a trade good, as the Sumerians had trade colonies as far away as Tell Brak in Syria since the Uruk period. The statuette is currently claimed to have been made in Mari, but there remains the possibility that there is some connection to Sumer.

Ur-Nanshe, King of Lagash, ruled c. 2520 BCE. Excavations at Lagash (modern-day Telloh) provided archaeologists with a massive number of cuneiform tablets. These tablets, together with inscriptions on monuments and stelae, provided important information about the Sumerian civilization during this period.

Kish was another important city-state in the Early Dynastic period. Kish was founded sometime around the Jemdet Nasr period. Although Kish was impacted by the flood of c. 2900 BCE, it flourished soon after. According to legend, the deities brought kingship down to Earth for a second time after the Great Flood and established it in Kish. Modern scholars first confirmed the title for a king, *lugal* (big man), as opposed to the previous *en* (priest) or *en-lugal* (priest-king), in the records from Kish.

Part of Kish's importance lay in its strategic position. It was situated where the Tigris and Euphrates come close together, so it had control over both rivers. Thus, the people could influence the irrigation waters and river traffic farther south; it was a powerful position that could affect the veritable lifeblood of the southern city-states.

Urbanization developed in the Uruk period, but it increased during the Early Dynastic periods. The Early Dynastic I period saw more innovative developments. New cities were built, and by the Early Dynastic II period, they had become city-states. The central buildings of these city-states were still religious buildings, which by this time were almost entirely ziggurats.

The city of Ur was founded during the Ubaid period. By the Early Dynastic period, it was a highly developed and prosperous city. Several other cities were on par with Ur, and these cities developed into fully-fledged independent city-states.

The city-states were similar in regards to cultural and political ideas and administration, yet they were undoubtedly heterogeneous and independent from each other. In previous eras, towns were recognized by other cities as major political entities, and there were periods when one held sway over others.

Each city-state consisted of a central city with surrounding smaller villages. They had their own armies, central food storage facilities, ziggurats, administrative centers, and specialized industries. They traded with each other, the neighboring world, and far afield.

Apart from the natural river shifts, human changes to the natural watercourses increased. The people diverted the rivers through canals, which had been done in previous eras as well. There are inscriptions from the late Early Dynastic III period, when writing was more developed, attesting to the large and important water diversions and canals. As mentioned above, a king of Lagash added how he honored the goddess Nanshe by building a canal to an inscription.

Conflicts, Battles, and Wars

Skirmishes are as old as the human race itself, and the Sumerians were no exception. As the city-states flourished and the populations grew, so did the need for more—more land, more resources, more control. The city-states also needed more protection against foreign enemies, such as the Gutians and the Elamites, who raided their trade routes and invaded their lands. Armies were created, weapons were developed, and cities were surrounded by defensive walls.

Battles were often fought between neighboring Sumerian city-states and included trade disputes, boundary disputes, resource control, and ownership matters. The conflicts driven by rivalry increased during the Early Dynastic period, which is reflected in the depictions of battles in artworks.

According to the Sumerian King List, rivalries led to battles, which then led to one city taking control of the other after defeating them. This meant the end of a line of kings, as the kingship of the conquered city was removed. Usually, the conquered city would eventually rebel and become autonomous again, thus kicking off a new dynasty.

The first pictographic depiction of a battle dates to around 3500 BCE, and it came from Kish. The first historically recorded war took place after c. 2700 BCE. This conflict was between the Sumerians and the Elamites. The king of Kish at the time, Enembaragesi, defeated the Elamites and carried off their weapons. The famous Stele of the Vultures records one of the many battles fought between the neighboring Sumerian city-states of Lagash and Umma, with this particular battle taking place sometime around 2500 BCE. Apart from the rather gruesome depiction of vultures carrying off the heads of the vanquished, this stele gives historians insight into the weapons and military formation of the victor: Lagash.

Cuneiform Script

During the Early Dynastic II period, clay seals were wider and elaborately decorated with human or animal scenes. The difference in clay seals is one of the few ways scholars distinguish between the Early Dynastic I and Early Dynastic II periods.

The most important invention during the Early Dynastic period is arguably the invention of writing. Cuneiform tablets with the same Archaic script have been found at several sites. These sites are far apart from each other, which indicates that the script did not develop in isolation. City-states were in continuous contact, and they would have shared ideas and inventions, despite their autonomy.

Example of pictographic script.
https://commons.wikimedia.org/wiki/File:Blau_Monument_British_Museum_86260.jpg

By c. 2700 BCE, the original pictographic script, also called proto-Sumerian or Archaic, had evolved to include representations of sounds. This enabled the Sumerians to write any word or even abstract concepts. By c. 2500 BCE, the script had developed into a limited number of wedge-shaped lines that could be arranged in various ways and combinations to transmit anything that needed to be communicated.

The script, which originated due to the need to record trade and administrative matters, bloomed into a full-blown written language. Toward the end of the Early Dynastic era, the Sumerians created literature.

Chapter 4 – The Akkadian Period

In the northern city of Kish during the 24th century BCE, a foundling raised by the king's gardener became the king's cupbearer. This king was Ur-Zababa. The position of cupbearer had to be filled by someone who was seen as trusted and powerful. Some scholars believe the cupbearer influenced the king's decisions. This cupbearer of Ur-Zababa would later become Sargon the Great.

At this time, the powerful king from Uruk in southern Sumer was Lugal-zage-si. He was in the process of expanding his territory, and his armies were working their way upriver to Kish. According to some sources, Lugal-zage-si had already conquered most of the Sumerian city-states and some areas adjacent to Sumer. Some scholars claim Lugal-zage-si oversaw the world's first empire, but this is refuted by evidence and analysis. It is accepted that Lugal-zage-si gained control over several city-states and then bragged that he had conquered all of Sumer. One must also remember that the fiercely independent city-states of ancient Sumer did not see their geographical locations as part of a whole—in other words, a country—despite having the same language and culture.

Ur-Zababa sent his cupbearer with a message to Lugal-zage-si, supposedly to offer a deal. It turns out that the message actually asked Lugal-zage-si to kill the messenger! Ur-Zababa must have lost his trust in his cupbearer at some point and wanted to get rid of him. Whether the message contained any suggestion of a peace deal is unclear. What is known is that Lugal-zage-si and Sargon joined forces and easily conquered Kish. Sargon became the king of Kish and then had a falling out with his benefactor. He captured Lugal-zage-si and cruelly forced him to wear a yoke around his neck. Sargon then dragged him to Nippur, the city-state of the deity Enlil, in whose name Lugal-zage-si claimed his kingship.

The former cupbearer to the king of Kish took the name Sargon (also spelled as Sarru-kin, which is believed to mean "the king is established/legitimate") as his throne name. According to legend and from Sargon's so-called autobiography, he was born to a priestess of an important temple and did not know his father. He was beloved and selected for kingship as a youth by the Sumerian goddess Inanna or, according to some sources, Ishtar. It must be noted that the records of this version of events date to the Old Babylonian period, which came much later. Thus, its authenticity as coming from Sargon himself must remain in doubt.

The Conquests of King Sargon

Sargon set out on a military expansion campaign across Sumer and later boasted in an inscription that he triumphed in thirty-four battles on his journey to the Persian Gulf. During his travels, he conquered the whole of Sumer. Thus, the first true empire in history was born. Sargon's reign lasted from c. 2334 BCE to 2279 BCE, and his successors ruled after him until the empire was overthrown in c. 2150 BCE.

According to some sources, the socio-political situation in Sumer was not as bright as it had been. The elite and priesthood were abusing their power to the extent that the lower classes were suffering unbelievable hardships. Some are said to have been forced to sell their children to cover their debts. In some states, the rulers became nothing more than warlords ruling with an iron fist. The struggles of the commoners against their elite rulers may have contributed to Sargon's successes.

To the east, the conquest of an Elamite city, Arawa, was recorded in inscriptions, and other Elamite cities followed, although we do not know the exact years or names. On a victory stele found in Susa, Sargon calls himself the conqueror of Elam and Parabium. This might indicate that he had fully conquered Elam to the east of Sumer and Akkad. To the north of Akkad in the Upper Euphrates region, there is evidence of Sargon's conquests in archaeological and textual records. At Mari, for example, the great palace was destroyed shortly after the beginning of Sargon's reign and then later rebuilt during the middle of the Akkadian period. Sargon also made an inscription stating that Mari and Elam obeyed him as the lord of the land.

Some of the wars fought during Sargon's reign appear to be raids rather than a war of conquest. In addition, many of the foreign regions were city-states rather than countries. Sargon's trade ambitions may have been satisfied by having merchants installed in some foreign countries rather than governors.

Many Sargonic inscriptions are known today only through copies made by later Babylonian scribes. From this information, modern-day scholars have ascertained that Sargon indeed conquered and made incursions into most of the ancient Near East. He called himself "king of the world" and the king and/or priest of various areas. One inscription reads that Dagan (the chief deity of several ancient Near East nations) gave Sargon Mari, Yarmuti, Ebla (Irbil), and as far as the cedar forests and the silver mountains. The latter probably indicates Lebanon and the Taurus Mountains.

Sargon created a new capital called Agade to the north of Sumer, and his empire was called the Akkadian Empire. The people of the lands forming Akkad north of the Sumerian city-states were mostly

Semitic-speaking tribes. Under the new centralized administration, the official language was Akkadian, although they used the Sumerian cuneiform script. The various languages and dialects of conquered states were still in use, but preference was given to Akkadian, which eventually became the lingua franca of the ancient Near East.

Although the general opinion of later ancient records states that Sargon built his new capital of Agade or Akkad, there are tantalizing clues that the city already existed before Sargon came to power. The earliest written mention of the city can be found during the Second Dynasty of Uruk, dating to the so-called "year date" of Ensakusanna.

The location of Agade remains elusive to this day. The Akkadians undoubtedly inherited their penchant for recording commercial transactions, personal and administrative matters, building projects, trade and trading partners, skirmishes and wars, and religious matters from the Sumerians. The discovery of Agade and its archives will shed light on and clarify much of this period.

The Wealthy Capital of the Akkadian Empire: Agade

The capital of the Akkadian Empire is described in contemporary and copied materials from other Mesopotamian sources as a wealthy, thriving, and bustling metropolis. It had an especially busy harbor. Ships at the docks were described as loading and offloading agricultural produce, various trade goods, scarce resources, and exotic goods from distant lands. The conquest of Sumer opened the route to the Persian Gulf, so all the sea and river trade crafts now docked at Agade. Sea traffic came from Bahrain, the Indus Valley, Egypt, Arabia, and Ethiopia.

Legends of the city's riches and treasures circulated long after it was gone. In later periods, it was a destination for treasure hunters. Extant texts, for instance, describe a three-year-long archaeological excavation undertaken by a scribe during the time of Babylonian King Nabonidus, who ruled c. 555 BCE to 539 BCE.

Sargon wanted to extend trade and diplomatic relationships from his capital city across the entire ancient Near East. Sargon's armies were said to have marched as far as the Mediterranean, Syria, Anatolia, the sources of the Tigris and Euphrates, and areas around the Arabian Gulf, conquering all in their path. Sargon controlled most of the trade routes across the ancient Near East.

Much of Sargon's rule has become so intertwined with legends that it is difficult to discern fact from fiction. Sargon was a legend in his own time, and rulers of other kingdoms and later eras would claim descendancy to Sargon's lineage to legitimize their rule or gain higher standing and respect.

The Semitic Akkadians had mingled with and learned from the Sumerians over a long period of time, and Sargon's new empire flourished with the new additional territories, his new capital city, and a new centralized government. The brilliant Sargon realized that the fiercely independent Sumerian city-states would soon be clamoring for their independence once more. As a countermeasure, he installed family members and trusted leaders in various prominent positions in the cities. Nevertheless, part of his army was kept busy putting down recurring revolts, especially toward the end of his reign.

After unifying the south of Mesopotamia, Sargon conquered the rest of the loosely associated cities in ancient Mesopotamia and other regions of the ancient Near East. The chronology and the exact extent of these conquests remain elusive. It appears that battles in distant places were not followed up with the continued rule of that state; it is possible these battles were brief military follow-up incursions to subdue the areas that tried to regain independence. Records from cities like Mari, Ebla, and others confirm Sargon's conquests and influence across the Fertile Crescent and beyond. Tablets from Ebla indicate that it was a province of Akkad at one time.

Akkad – A Centralized Imperial Government

Local governors across the Akkadian Empire were appointed by Sargon, and they implemented the policies dictated by the central government in Agade. Standard units of measure and tax systems were implemented across the empire.

The implemented policies and changes included overhauling and centralizing the administration of agricultural production. Agricultural lands were enlarged by relocating people to nearby urban centers, thus centralizing the labor force. These newly extended urban centers were enclosed by city walls. Agricultural production from the dry fields in the north of Mesopotamia was supplemented with irrigation.

Part of Sargon's strategy to limit revolts included relocating Akkadian people to Sumerian and other city-states. He used propaganda to keep people in awe of him by describing wars, detailing the number of enemies slain and the number of people enslaved during campaigns. These records were inscribed on statues and stelae. Revolts were brutally crushed, and entire cities were punished by tearing down their city walls. In southern Mesopotamia, that meant flooding the cities with river water. The people who remained loyal to the Akkadian Empire during revolts were rewarded with land taken from the rebels and the slain.

Art from the Akkadian period shows a marked swing to more naturalistic scenes, monumental art, and sculpture. Seals were created with backgrounds and realistic drawings of people and animals. Sculptures and reliefs portrayed real people, which is evident from the remains of similar, if not identical, representations of kings placed in the temple precincts of many cities across the empire. It can be assumed that these statues served as a constant reminder to the people of who the king was. Like the statues of the patron deities, the statues of the king were always present in cities.

A magnificent bronze head, which is thought to have been part of a statue, was recovered during excavations at Nineveh in 1931. It is believed to portray Sargon of Akkad. Bronze statues were cast by the lost wax technique, in which the melted metal was cast in a wax mold. The Akkadian kings used visual arts, including statues of themselves with inscriptions of their deeds and religious devotion, as a propaganda device.

The Akkadian Empire gave us the first "named" poet in history! Enheduanna was a princess and a high priestess, and she wrote poems and hymns during the reign of Sargon the Great. She was actually Sargon's daughter. Luckily, her literary contributions formed part of the later Old Babylonian and Assyrian scribal curriculums, so copies of her work were saved for posterity.

As part of Sargon's strategic appointments after he conquered Sumer, Sargon appointed his daughter, Enheduanna, as the high priestess of the patron deity of Ur in southern Mesopotamia. It is speculated that the appointment was partly to link the Semitic religion of Akkad to the Sumerian religion. Sargon did not replace the Sumerian gods; he adopted them into the Akkadian culture, sometimes under Akkadian names. During Leonard Woolley's excavations at Ur, he discovered an alabaster disc that named Enheduanna as the high priestess of the Sumerian moon god, Inanna. It also stated that Sargon was her father.

Rimush - The Usurper

When Sargon died after ruling for around fifty-five years, his younger son, Rimush, became the ruler. Why Rimush became the ruler and not Sargon's eldest son is a mystery. Conquered states saw Sargon's death as a chance to get their autonomy back, so rebellions broke out across the empire.

Rimush gathered his father's forces and brutally crushed the rebels. He dealt harshly with the Sumerian city-states. Mass deportations and seizure of lands were the order of the day. Temple lands, which were the primary source of income for priests, were confiscated and given to Akkadians. According to records recovered from Umma, survivors from rebellions and other deportees were put in labor camps and worked to death. Could concentration camps be counted as another Sumerian first?

Victory stelae of Rimush have been found in several places, including Elam. He called himself "king of the world" and "king of the universe." And like his father, he inscribed the exact numbers of soldiers and civilians killed, deported, and enslaved. One inscription, for instance, at the city of Kazallu, where a rebellion had broken out, recorded that twelve thousand people were killed in battle and that five thousand were taken as slaves. Inscriptions also recorded the types and quantities of booty confiscated by the king's forces.

Rimush only ruled for nine turbulent years before he was assassinated in his palace. According to legend, he was strangled with cylinder seals, which were probably tied in a string. The culprits were never identified, but speculation includes his older brother, Manishtushu.

Manishtushu – Rightful Heir of Sargon?

Manishtushu declared that Enlil, one of the Sumerian chief deities, had called him to kingship. After the continuous wars of his brother's short reign, he arranged a feast in Agade for representatives of various cities and regions. Legend has it that a total of 964 rulers gathered at Agade for a lavish feast, with beer flowing abundantly. Manishtushu's guards and soldiers looked on to prevent skirmishes from breaking out. Manishtushu managed to convince them to accept a land deal. The details of it are not clear, but it was highly favorable to Manishtushu. The beer probably helped!

Nevertheless, Manishtushu tried to promote peace, unlike his brother before him. He appears to have had peaceful trade relations with cities and states in the Iranian desert, Anatolia, the Mediterranean region, the Indus Valley, Arabia, Egypt, and perhaps Ethiopia.

Records recovered at Tell Brak in Syria detail large-scale land reforms, which were done under the military's supervision. The most important stele from this period is the Manishtushu Obelisk. This magnificent object was made from black diorite stone imported from ancient Magan (Oman). It details the king's gift to four officials. An inscription states that Manishtushu sent a fleet of ships to Magan and successfully fought against thirty-two cities that had gathered to fight his forces. He destroyed their cities "as far as the silver mines."

Manishtushu, like his brother Rimush, was assassinated in Agade by members of his court.

Naram-Sin – Classical Period

The third ruler of Akkad was Manishtushu's son, Naram-Sin. The Akkadian Empire reached its peak during his reign. He was a rather controversial figure according to later sources, and he was blamed in *The Curse of Agade* for being responsible for the empire's fall. Like his grandfather, Sargon, Naram-Sin was ruthless at times but also the epitome of a true warrior king.

Naram-Sin recorded an inscription about a revolt of Sumerian cities led by Uruk and Kish. The inscription recounts that Naram-Sin fought nine battles at the beginning of his reign. The goddess Ishtar helped him to be victorious, and his people asked him to become the god of the city of Agade, where he built a temple for himself. Protective walls were demolished, cities were flooded, and many of the captives were brutally killed and enslaved.

Naram-Sin's reign is known as the Classical period of the Akkadian Empire due to its magnificent art and the size and achievements reached during this time. He expanded the empire to include the Zagros Mountains and their rich mineral resources and also possibly Cyprus. A destruction layer at Ebla in Syria dates to Naram-Sin's reign.

A cylinder seal depicts hunting scenes with Naram-Sin, which may indicate that he did not accompany his troops everywhere or that wars and conflicts tapered down sometimes.

Naram-Sin was credited with many building projects. He demolished the temple of Enlil in Nippur and replaced it with a larger and elaborately decorated temple. The majestic project was overseen by his son. There is a detailed account of the building materials, the progression of the work, and the numbers of different craftsmen, like carpenters, sculptors, metal workers, and more. The best craftsmen were commandeered from every corner of the empire to complete this temple.

At some point in his reign, Naram-Sin started to look at himself as a demi-god and is portrayed with the horned helmet that was once reserved for depicting deities. This can be seen, for example, on the famous pink limestone Victory Stele of Naram-Sin, which was originally from Sippar but discovered in Susa. Today, it is on display in the Louvre in Paris.

It is generally believed that an ancient treaty between the Egyptians and the Hittites after the Battle of Kadesh was the first treaty in the world. However, it is possible that the peace treaty was yet another first for Mesopotamia. It was concluded between Akkad and Elam during Naram-Sin's reign. It appears that he made a peace treaty with an Elamite king named Khita. The king of Elam stated that the enemy of Naram-Sin would be his enemy and that the friend of Naram-Sin would also be his friend. The treaty was sealed by the marriage of Naram-Sin to Khita's daughter.

Naram-Sin ruled for thirty-six years and died of natural causes around 2218 BCE.

Shar-Kali-Sharri

After Naram-Sin's death, his son, Shar-Kali-Sharri, became king. Yet again, the transition of power presented an opportunity for the Sumerian city-states to regain their independence. Shar-Kali-Sharri put down these revolts, and scholars are often forced to piece together bits and pieces of his twenty-five-year reign from records of year names. These include references such as the year in which Shar-Kali-Sharri captured Sarlagab, the king of Gutium, or the year Shar-Kali-Shari laid the foundation of the temple.

It is clear that the nomadic Gutians, who came from the foothills of the Zagros Mountains, intensified their incursions into the Akkadian territories. They were a menace during Naram-Sin's reign. Shar-Kali-Sharri collected high taxes from the empire to keep his armies equipped and ready to fight these incursions. This led to increased uprisings in the states under his rule. It was a vicious cycle, and he could not subdue every revolt, leading to the once-mighty Akkadian Empire losing control over much of its territory.

The End of an Empire

It behooves us to quote the author of the Sumerian King List at this point: "Then, who was king? Who was not king? Igigi, Nanum, Imi, and Elulu, the four of them were kings but ruled for a total of only 3 years."

Sargon and his dynasty connected the entire ancient Near East, allowing these regions to trade and exchange ideas. It seems that the Akkadians and Sumerians traveled in person to many parts of the inhabited world without playing the middleman as in pre-Sargonic times. Imports from outside the ancient Near East were recovered from the Akkadian era, and horses were imported for the first time, which could mean they had contact with people from the Eurasian Steppe.

The Akkadian language remained the lingua franca, especially for international correspondence, for millennia to come.

More recent studies show that there are indications of severe droughts and other climatic changes, like lower levels of the vital rivers, which contributed to the demise of the Akkadian Empire. It stands to reason that a slump in food production would have increased internal riots and general unrest across much of the ancient Near East beginning around 2200 BCE.

The Gutians seized their opportunity.

This mask is thought to be of Sargon the Great.
Hans Ollermann, CC BY-SA 2.0 https://creativecommons.org/licenses/by-sa/2.0 via Wikimedia Commons; https://commons.wikimedia.org/wiki/File:Mask_of_Sargon_of_Akkad.jpg

Chapter 5 – The Gutian Period

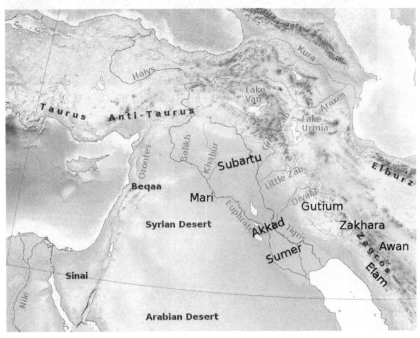

Map showing the Near East mountainous region.

Where Did the Gutians Come From?

The Gutians were uncultured tribes that came from the Zagros Mountains, at least according to the Sumerians. They were in the habit of conducting quick raids into cities and towns across ancient Mesopotamia from early on. Records of the period are scarce, and much of what is available was written before and after the Gutian period. Since they were always a thorn in the side of the civilized cities of Sumer and Akkad, as well as other settled folks across much of Mesopotamia, a certain skepticism should be applied to the often-biased information in these texts.

According to the well-known Sumerologist Thorkild Jacobsen, the Gutians ruled for around one hundred years. They do not appear to have left much of an impression on Sumerian culture, language, or development. The period was described by later scribes as the "dark ages." The uneducated Gutians had no idea how to run an advanced society and were blamed for the disintegration of the irrigation systems, famine, great hardships, and the decline of the entire region.

Many of the accusations heaped upon the Gutians may, in reality, be the result of a severe drought. The earlier invasions of the Gutians consisted of quick raids to obtain whatever they wanted. They would then return to their homeland in the foothills of the Zagros Mountains. However, their pattern suddenly shifted. Their motives had changed. They came down to Sumer with no intention of leaving again. They may have been driven into Mesopotamia by other factors. Moreover, the instability of the Akkadian Empire provided them with the right momentum for a full-scale invasion.

What Was the Gutian Strategy?

The Gutian raids had turned into conquests, destroying much in their path. They now occupied the areas that they invaded and installed their own rulers.

Evidence confirms widespread, severe, and centuries-long droughts and climate change across much of the ancient Near East; no explanation has yet been established for why this took place. This could have been the instigator of the Gutian invasion—pastoralists looking for greener pastures. It is thought that climate change occurred roughly from 2200 to 1900 BCE. It is possible a large volcanic eruption took place, but no culprit has been identified. It is clear, though, that there was desertification of once-fertile areas and a significant drop in rainfall in the rest of the ancient Near East, with widespread food shortages, unrests, revolts, wars, and massive movements of people. The severe drought is confirmed by sediment samples from seabeds, riverbeds, and even ancient Egyptian records from the time of Pharaoh Pepi II.

Some of the Sumerian city-states seem to have had some amount of authority left, albeit as underlings of Gutian rulers. Thus, they went on with certain projects in their cities while acknowledging their lower status by not calling themselves kings. For example, in Umma, an inscription states the prince or governor (*patesi* in Sumerian) built a temple in the time of S'ium (or Ba-s'ium), King of the Gutians.

The Sumerian city-state of Lagash (modern Telloh) thrived around 2144 during the so-called "dark ages." Their ruler, Gudea, called himself *ensi* and believed himself to be the shepherd of his people rather than their king. Inscriptions call him the *ensi* of the god Ningirsu. He built many temples in several of the Sumerian cities, including the city-state of Lagash. The most famous of these temples is called E-ninnu in the city of Girsu, which Gudea rebuilt after having a dream of being instructed by the gods to do so. Gudea professed that he devoted his life to pleasing the gods, especially Ningirsu, the patron deity of Lagash.

During Gudea's reign, irrigation, roads, and other old Sumerian systems were repaired and used again. He had trade connections with several foreign lands, as can be seen from the materials used in temple construction and decoration, which included ebony from the Indus Valley, stone from Oman, and cedar wood from Lebanon.

The several slightly different extant Sumerian King List contains the names of twenty-one to twenty-five Gutian rulers, of which very few can be verified. It was indeed a dark age with few cultural achievements, except for those produced in semi-autonomous cities by remnants of the previous cultures. Some scholars believe the Gutians blended into the Sumerian and Akkadian cultures over time. Eventually, they worshiped the same deities and assumed Akkadian names.

The semi-autonomous city-states managed their partial freedom by paying tribute to the Gutian state. They carried on with their usual pursuits, and some localized Gutians adopted their practices. Like their predecessors—the Akkadians—the Gutians were unable to keep control over the vast geographical area that once was under the control of the Akkadian Empire.

Uruk also appeared to be thriving under a succession of its own kings, although it was a vassal state of the Gutians. It is clear that in some Sumerian city-states, power and independence were building, as the inept Gutians failed to retain control. It was only a matter of time before they would fall.

Tablet bearing an inscription of the governor of Umma declaring he erected a temple during the reign of king S'ium or Ba-s'ium of Gutium.

Did the Gutians Leave Their Mark on Sumer?

As the Gutians' control declined further, a powerful king came to power in the city-state of Uruk. His name was Utu-hengal (also spelled as Utu-hegal). After making offers and supplications to the gods, he started a revolt against the Gutian rule. The Gutians gathered their forces to attack Utu-hengal, but he still triumphed. The king of the Gutians, Tirigan, fled to the Zagros Mountains. He and his family were taken prisoner by Utu-hengal's envoy. He was then returned to Utu-hengal blindfolded and with his hands in stocks.

Tirigan pleaded for mercy. Utu-hengal replied by putting his foot on Tirigan's neck. Sumerian kingship was restored to Uruk. Utu-hengal died seven years later in an accident. His son-in-law, Ur-Nammu, who was already the king of Ur, became king of Uruk as well. Thus, the next period in the history of Sumer, the Ur III Dynasty, began.

Seated King Ur-Nammu on a cylinder seal.
Steve Harris, source, CC BY-SA 2.0 https://creativecommons.org/licenses/by-sa/2.0 via Wikimedia Commons; https://commons.wikimedia.org/wiki/File:King_Ur-Nammu.jpg

Chapter 6 – The Sumerian Renaissance

There are more than 120,000 known cuneiform tablets from the following period of Sumerian history, of which many thousands still have to be deciphered. Much of the information so far deciphered is about administrative matters, transaction records, economic matters, trade, and food.

The Reign of Ur-Nammu

Ur-Nammu became the king of Ur around 2112 BCE. After inheriting the throne of Uruk from his father-in-law, Utu-hengal, Ur-Nammu founded the Ur III Dynasty (also known as the Neo-Sumerian Empire). He amalgamated the city-states of Ur, Uruk, and Eridu and then set out to liberate the other Sumerian city-states from the Gutians. He was an enlightened ruler, and he portrayed himself as a liberator rather than a conqueror when he attacked these city-states. Consequently, the inhabitants were more than willing to join the Neo-Sumerian Empire after Ur-Nammu drove the ruling Gutians out of their cities.

He incorporated the rest of Sumer and went on to conquer the middle and north of Mesopotamia by defeating the king of Elam, Puzur-Inshushinak. This Elamite king or his father before him had taken over territories in the middle and north of Mesopotamia since the Gutians were declining in power. Ur-Nammu also brought Elamite territories like Susa under Sumerian control.

During Ur-Nammu's reign, the city-states of Sumer were united as a cohesive whole under a Sumerian ruler for the first time. They had learned from the Akkadian Empire that a centralized rule and administration could be a powerful deterrent and strong defense against enemy attacks. Ur-Nammu claimed the title of king of Sumer and Akkad, as well as king of the four corners of the world. His propaganda included a return to the old ways—the good old days of freedom before the Akkadian Empire ruled the Sumerians with an iron fist.

Ur-Nammu reinstated the use of Sumerian as the official language and promoted cultural growth in art and literature. Ancient Sumerian epics, hymns, and poems were learned and recited in public.

Ur-Nammu is the first ruler whose recorded laws and punishments are preserved in writing. His law code included both public and civil laws. To the surprise of scholars, many of the punishments included fines to compensate the victims. Serious offenses like murder and rape did carry the death penalty, though.

After ruling for eighteen years, Ur-Nammu was killed in a battle against the invading Gutians. It appears his troops deserted him. Ur-Nammu's praises were still sung, and his deeds were probably exaggerated by later generations. He was honored as a god after his death.

A poet described Ur-Nammu's death and funeral. He talked about how Ur-Nammu's body was brought back to Ur on a bier and laid in his palace while his soldiers and widow mourned. It also laments the actions of the gods, who callously let him die. Other gods could only watch and wail. According to the poet, the funeral procession included a boat being broken and sunk to take Ur-Nammu to the underworld.

King Shulgi

Ur-Nammu's son, Shulgi, became his successor. Under his reign, the Ur III Dynasty hit its peak. The government was running smoothly, and taxation on the distribution of goods and services was perfectly planned and administered. Every city was responsible for paying taxes once a year, each in a different month, to maintain the state administration, public services, and military. Taxes were paid in the form of supplies, which were delivered to a central redistribution point.

From the corpus of extant documents dating to the Ur III period, scholars learned that an entire city was built to accommodate the central administration. This city was discovered near Nippur, which was considered the religious capital of Sumer. This storage and distribution city was called Puzrish-Dagan. Archaeologists discovered a multitude of tablets there, and it appears as if every item that entered or left the city was recorded and filed.

Shulgi's military campaigns included areas north, east, and west of Sumer, although these campaigns were often a result of rebellions. These were all recorded in detail on clay tablets and in inscriptions on statues and stelae.

Local authorities administered each city according to the regulations laid down by the central government in Ur. The head or prince of a locale functioned similarly to today's prime ministers. He reported to the king in Ur.

The head of the local authority was assisted in his duties by an *ensi* or governor, as well as a general (*shagina* in Sumerian), who was the head of the local military. Each city was responsible for its own planning, budgeting, administrative functions, and distribution operations, which were all done according to the central government's instructions.

All civil servants were expected to attend a school, where they learned their jobs, which included bookkeeping, weights and measurements, the calendar, and other scribal skills.

The central authorities standardized the types and sizes of bricks and even provided building plans in some cases. Kings paid for the construction of huge ziggurats in almost every city.

Shulgi's reign was plagued by incursions and battles against neighbors, nomads, and illegal immigrants. The same could be said of almost every state in the ancient Near East. There is evidence from this period that provides clues for major droughts, food shortages, and their inevitable consequences, which included mass migrations.

There is also enough confirmation in the records to prove that trade and diplomatic relationships and treaties were forged throughout the Ur III period. Some were broken or unilaterally changed before the clay was even dry. Relationships were enhanced by marriages and other family connections.

Ur III rulers also had to suppress internal revolts. Shulgi ruled for forty-seven years before he was killed in battle. Scholars have found all the year names of Shulgi's reign, and much information can be extrapolated from that. He wrote or commissioned many praise hymns and poems about himself. From his twenty-third regnal year onward, he had a sign for divinity added in front of his name, which meant that he claimed godhood from then on.

Later accounts were not as kind to Shulgi as he was to himself. The *Weidner Chronicle*—correspondence from a later ruler of Isin to a king of Babylon—states that the Gutians triumphed over Ur III because Shulgi and his father had disrespected the Babylonian god Marduk and other deities. Shulgi did not follow the religious rites properly when placating the deities, which was a grave sin at the time. According to this chronicle, Shulgi, his father, and his son changed some religious rules, which proved offensive to the gods.

Descendants of King Shulgi

Shulgi's son, Amar-Sin, succeeded him and reigned from c. 2046 to 2037 BCE. He also claimed divine status when he was king. His name even means "immortal moon god" (Sin was the name of the moon god of Sumer).

Amar-Sin coped with the same issues and projects that his father had before him. There are extant records of all the year names of Amar-Sin. From those, it is clear that he engaged in military actions almost every year, even more than once in some years.

Amar-Sin apparently died from a foot infection or scorpion bite and was succeeded by his son, Shu-Sin. Shu-Sin reigned for nine years, all of which are known via the year names. In the fourth year of his reign, he was plagued by the Amorites. He had a wall constructed between the Euphrates and Tigris Rivers to block them from coming farther south.

Many artifacts with Shu-Sin's name or inscriptions have been unearthed. A so-called love poem referring to Shu-Sin is probably the most widely known. It was discovered in the ruins of Nippur and translated by well-known Sumerologist Samuel Noah Kramer. Scholars associate it with the ancient annual celebration of the divine marriage between Dumuzi and Inanna, where the king portrays Dumuzi as the bridegroom, and a high priestess takes the part of Inanna as the bride. Similar love poems are present across the ancient Near East, and it is also compared to the Song of Songs in the Christian Bible.

The long reign of Ibbi-Sin, the son and successor of Shu-Sin, lasted from 2028 to 2004 BCE. He was the last ruler of Ur III. The dynasty was in decline throughout most of his reign, and by the end, the empire only consisted of Ur and its surroundings.

The Unrelenting Amorites

The main culprits were the Amorites. The wall built by Shu-Sin across the divide between the Tigris and Euphrates proved totally inadequate to keep the Amorites out. The internal unrest, riots, and declarations of independence by previously conquered states were widespread across Mesopotamia and beyond. Invaders were assisted by their kin already dwelling in the lands of Sumer and Akkad.

Around 2004 BCE, the unrelenting Elamites, together with other mountain tribes from the Zagros range, attacked the city of Ur. They destroyed much of the city and took Ibbi-Sin as a prisoner back to Elam, where he later died. The demise of the city and dynasty is lamented in an elegy by an unknown composer.

Chapter 7 – The Decline of Sumer

The Origin of the Amorites

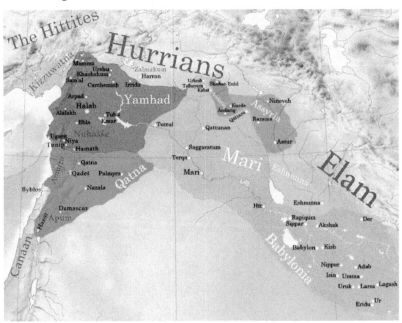

Map showing various Amorite states and Assyria, c. 1764 BCE.
Attar-Aram syria, CC BY-SA 4.0 https://creativecommons.org/licenses/by-sa/4.0 via Wikimedia Commons; https://commons.wikimedia.org/wiki/File:Third_Mari.png

Scholars agree that the Amorites came from the Levant. It is further agreed that the Amorites were originally nomadic people who infiltrated communities as they traveled and posed threats to previously settled groups. These nomadic tribes were governed by chieftains who decided their routes, trade, and invasions of settlements. At some time, the name "Amorite" was given to a specific group of Semitic people who, although nomadic and at times semi-nomadic, lived from the land and took what they wanted from settlements they came across. As this tribe grew bigger, stronger, and more adept at taking what they wanted from others, they acquired land and became a threat to the already developed city-states in the neighboring regions.

The Amorites were called "Amorites" on tablets from the northwest, such as the Ebla archives, where a transaction is recorded as being paid for with "Amorite silver." Tablets from Mari also refer to the Amorites. To the early Sumerians, all the lands to the west were known as the lands of the Martu—their name for the Amorites. The name "Amurru" was the Akkadian word used to talk about this disruptive group of people. It also denoted their geographic and linguistic origins.

At the start of the 2nd millennium, large tribal groups of the Amurru migrated from Arabia and permanently occupied Mesopotamia. They settled in small groups and took on a way of life similar to that of the Sumerians and Akkadians. Most scholars posit that this infiltration was connected to the earlier sources that describe the Amorites, while others claim that these people were Canaanites.

One of the cities that was linked to the Amorites is Mari, modern-day Tell Hariri in Syria. At this site, many clay tablets were excavated that had the same Paleo-Canaanite script that scholars attribute to the Semitic inhabitants. Some scholars even believe that Mari was part of an Amorite kingdom. According to historians, the later King Hammurabi of Babylon was a descendent of the Amorites.

Cuneiform clay tablets from the Amorite Kingdom of Mari. Dated to the beginning of the 2nd millennium BCE.

Gary Todd, CC0, via Wikimedia Commons;
https://commons.wikimedia.org/wiki/File:Cuneiform_Clay_Tablets_from_Amorite_Kingdom_of_Ma
ri,_1st_Half_of_2nd_Mill._BC.jpg

The Constant Threat of the Amorites

The Amorites were known to be fierce and unwavering warriors. They were led by their chieftains and posed a threat to any settlement or city-state that they wanted to loot. This included taking lands for their herds to graze. They were said to have been a dominant force feared by the Sumerians, for they were as brave as they were violent in battle. Clay tablets in Akkadian describe the Amorites and their way of life as repugnant and revolting.

The Amorites were known across the Levant. They were called Martu by the Sumerians, Amurru by the Akkadians, and Amar by the Egyptians. They were represented in Egyptian frescoes as having light hair, fair skin, blue eyes, and pointed beards. Their facial features were dominated by a large, curved nose.

The Amorites were considered barbarians by most of the nations they came across; thus, they are usually described in negative terms, such as the following example from the Sumerians:

"The MARTU who know no grain...The MARTU who know no house nor town, the boors of the mountains...The MARTU who digs up truffles...who does not bend his knees [to cultivate the land], who eats raw meat, who has no house during his lifetime, who is not buried after death."[1]

The Amorites were a constant menace to the Akkadian and Sumerian city-states. Chieftains of the Amorite tribes established their settlements in Mari, Qatna, Yamhad, and Assur. They became urbanized while still remaining a force to be reckoned with. The Babylonians had a very famous king called Hammurabi, who is usually, although incorrectly, credited with creating the first written law code in history. (Ur-Nammu created the oldest surviving law code so far discovered.) The stele of Hammurabi found at a site in Diyarbekir claims that Hammurabi was "The King of the Amorites." Thus, scholars have concluded that Hammurabi was an Amorite who ascended the Babylonian throne after Sin-Muballit, who was also an Amorite.

The Amorites were not content with the cities they had invaded in Mesopotamia. They continued their conquest to the north of Canaan up to Kadesh. The Paleo-Semitic language of the Amorites blended well with the Semitic language of the Akkadians, which became the dominant spoken and written language (lingua franca) of the ancient Near East. Akkadian was used primarily until the latter part of the 2nd millennium BCE.

---

[1] *Sumerian Texts of Varied Contents*, Chiera, Edward, Published by University of Chicago Press, Chicago, 1954.

Sumerian Defensive Tactics against the Amorites

King Shulgi, son of King Ur-Nammu, constructed a defensive wall at Ur to stop the invasion of the barbaric tribes known as the Martu in Sumerian (the Amurru of the Akkadians and Amorites of the later Hebrews). This wall was built along the eastern border of his kingdom to defend against the Amorites, who had already taken control of some other Sumerian city-states.

This wall was 155 miles (249.45 kilometers) long, according to the records of its construction. During Shulgi's reign, the wall kept the Elamites from invading the kingdom. This was due to extra fortifications that were added by Shulgi. Unfortunately, the design of the wall didn't include watchtowers or foot holders for defenders. (Foot holders allowed soldiers to see over the wall while still being protected.) This essentially meant that anyone could walk around at either end of the wall before they were seen.

After the death of King Shulgi, his son and heir, Amar-Sin, reevaluated the wall construction and added further fortifications. However, the wall was too long and could not be guarded efficiently. Another factor that led to Ur's eventual fall was that during Shulgi's reign, some nomadic Amorite tribes had already found their way around the wall and established settlements within the region.

Shu-Sin, the younger brother of Amar-Sin, also attempted to strengthen the defensive wall originally built by his grandfather, but the raids from both external and internal Amorite tribes made his efforts futile. Once his son, Ibbi-Sin, ascended the throne, the once-majestic kingdom was lost. The Third Dynasty of Ur was a mere glimmer of its former glory and reduced to a basic city-state.

The Weakened Sumerian Empire Attacked by the Elamites

The systematic, almost strategically planned Amorite invasion of the Sumerian Empire weakened this once-great empire to such an extent that it became ripe for attack by the Elamites.

Babylonian inscriptions confirm that the Amorites already had a strong foothold in some Syrian cities. By ransacking city after city in Sumer and conquering Babylon, which became their capital, the Amorites succeeded in bringing down a civilization that had developed over centuries. This civilization had the most innovative minds of the time and a strong character. Its people developed a complex society, religion, culture, and art, and it was conquered by uncivilized, ununified barbarians, at least according to ancient texts.

Famine Further Weakens Ur

Geologist Matt Konfrist stated at a conference of the American Geophysical Union that geological records showed an extended drought in ancient Sumer that began around 2200 BCE. He posits this drought was caused by evaporation changes from both the Red Sea and the Dead Sea, which caused lower rainfall throughout the region. The drought caused famine across the entire ancient Near East. It affected the Sumerian Empire, as the people greatly depended on irrigation from the flooding rivers—rivers that now were not filled with annual melting snow at their sources.

The Ur III Dynasty was already in a state of decline due to the widespread and persistent invasions by the Amorites. The combination of drought, famine, and invasion effectively brought this magnificent civilization to the brink of collapse.

Another factor that influenced the decline and ultimate collapse of Ur and other Sumerian city-states is that during times of drought, famine, or invasion, people living in outlying smaller cities or farmers affected severely by these factors inevitably migrated to the larger cities in search of work and food. This caused a strain on the urban economy and infrastructure.

Deciphered administrative documents from the Ur III period shows that during Ibbi Sin's seventh and eighth year of rule, the price of grain increased by 60 percent. This increase was undoubtedly caused by the combined factors of the drought and the Amorite attacks on farmers and lands.

As time went by, the architectural marvel of the 150-mile-long defensive wall fell into a state of disrepair. The once-wealthy kingdom was plagued by economic woes due to overpopulation and Amorites who usurped cities that once paid tribute to Ur in the form of money, grain, or livestock. Ur was weakened and impoverished during Ibbi-Sin's reign, making it ripe for the picking by the Elamites. Around this time, one of the king's high officials left the court and started his own small kingdom in the southern city of Isin.

The Elamites, led by Kindattu, finally attacked the city of Ur around 2004 BCE. According to some sources, the Elamites had formed a coalition with the Amorites. They ransacked the city and captured King Ibbi-Sin, the last Neo-Sumerian ruler. Records show that he was taken to the city of Elam as a prisoner. What became of him then and how he died remains unknown. On a clay tablet housed in the Louvre in Paris, the inscription states that King Ibbi-Sin would be taken to the city of Elam in fetters and that he would never return to his homeland.

The official who had started his own dynasty in Isin ruled over his tiny empire while the other cities broke off into their own city-states. The next two hundred years were a tumultuous era with constant wars between the city-states. Great lamentations were composed that bewailed the loss of support from the gods. It was believed the gods had allowed or even ordered the Elamites to destroy the great city of Ur and its prosperous empire.

The fall of Ur and the further decline of the Sumerian city-states caused the end of a civilization that is truly legendary. Today, this civilization is referred to as the "Origin of Civilization." The advancements the Sumerians made still affect our lives today—just look at your watch!

Chapter 8 – Sumerian Society and Famous Rulers

The societal structure of the Sumerian civilization evolved over the centuries. It adapted and changed in regard to the environment, settlements, and city-states. The inhabitants of the lands between the Tigris and Euphrates Rivers created magnificent innovations, such as an irrigation system. This also meant that people had to work together on a large scale for these innovations to be built, maintained, and function. A governing body had to be established to ensure that canals and ditches were dug, repaired, and directed to the fields, villages, and cities in a system that apportioned the water fairly. At the same time, the rivers' flooding had to be tamed by communal efforts to ensure the safety of people and property. Thus, a government was formed, and laws were developed that needed to be enforced.

Developing a Social Hierarchy in Sumer

Farmers of early Sumer considered the land they farmed as their property and not communal lands. Subsistence farming changed to overproduction due to the successful irrigation systems, and surplus food was shared and traded. This was the beginning of barter and trade systems. Farmers who had more land and better crop yields could become wealthy through trade. In the past, a farmer's extended family was used for labor, but the people realized this could be supplemented by external labor instead of working their fields alone as a family enterprise.

Some farmers were more successful than others and had a surplus of seeds and food. Farmers with a bad crop yield would likely approach wealthier farmers to borrow seed, agreeing to repay the lender with their next harvest. If their next harvest was also unsuccessful and they could not repay their loans, they would either be forced to surrender their land or become a laborer on the lands owned by the lending farmer.

Successful and abundant food production led to the specialization of crafts, such as pottery, weaving, tool making, and other industries. These events developed a social class hierarchy, where the upper class consisted of the farmers who employed laborers and did not work their own lands, administrators of communal endeavors, priests, and successful manufacturers of essential goods. The lower class was made up of laborers, some of whom were possibly former landowners but had lost their lands and were now laborers.

Upper-class inhabitants and those who could afford it also owned slaves that worked in their households or on their lands. Slaves were prisoners of war from other city-states. They were sold and bought at markets or exchanged between households or industries.

Class Distinctions

Essentially, the hierarchy was divided into four groups: the religious class, the upper class, the lower class, and the slaves. These class distinctions formed the framework of society for the ancient Sumerians.

Religious Class – Priests and priestesses were powerful. They seemed to have had the right to do as they pleased. It was often only by currying favor with the priests that people could approach the deities for blessings, as only the priests and priestesses could commune with the gods, interpret messages, and explain omens to the people. Priests also assumed the role of doctors in ancient Sumer. If a member of the family was sick, one would call on the help of a priest. A cuneiform tablet was found depicting two priests dressed like fish. They did this to better communicate with the water god to help heal a sick boy. Priests had to shave their hair as a form of reverence to the gods they served.

The Upper Class or Elites - Upper-class men wore jewelry, particularly rings. Their hair was long, and they had mustaches and long beards. Early on, their robes were a type of kilt, but they eventually became a full dress, going from shoulder to ankle. Women often wore off-the-shoulder dresses. Their long hair was braided and sometimes piled on top of their heads. During winter, people wore cloaks made from sheep's wool to keep out the cold.

The Lower Class - Ancient Sumerians paid laborers to perform tasks, such as working in the fields or running a shop. The lower-class people lived comfortably. They had homes, wore clothing they could afford, and sported jewelry made from shells or stones. The elite, on the other hand, wore gold. No law prevented lower-class men from moving up the social ladder.

Slavery - City-states that conquered other city-states captured prisoners. They were brought back and sold as slaves to the king, the temple, the elites, or whoever could afford to keep one. Slaves were bought and sold among citizens, and records of these transactions were recorded on clay tablets. Slaves tended to cost less than donkeys or cattle.

Women in Society

Women did not have the same rights as men in ancient Sumer. An example of inequality is stated in one of the Ur-Nammu law codes, where a woman caught in an adulterous event would be killed while the man got off scot-free! However, women could trade and buy and sell goods freely at the marketplace, own property, move where they wanted, and manage legal issues. Women also had the right to start businesses. Some women had jobs running sections of the city-states and other government jobs. Upper-class women or members of the royal family could decide to become priestesses. Women in city-states that had a female patron deity were highly respected.

Sumerian women could become scribes, priestesses, doctors, and judges. The women were the prime beer brewers, which was an important job. A lady beer brewer or innkeeper named Kubaba or Ku Bau was even honored with the kingship of the important city-state of Kish.

Rulers of the City-States

Sumerian settlements developed into city-states, and each city-state had a patron deity. The temples of the city-state reflected the city's wealth. The more majestic and magnificent the temple was, the more powerful and wealthy the king would appear to others.

Clay cuneiform tablet of the Sumerian King List.

The Controversial Sumerian King List

Several cuneiform clay tablets have been found across Sumerian city-states from their later periods that describe the ancient rulers as godlike humans. At some point during the last phase of the Sumerian civilization, a list of all the Sumerian kings from the beginning of the Sumerian kingship was compiled. The controversial Sumerian King List details kings that ruled for tens of thousands of years. It is considered by scholars to be a combination of reality and mythology. The Sumerian King List contains around twenty fragments of clay tablets. The main fragment was excavated in Nippur, but discoveries were made at other ancient sites, such as Susa, Adab, Sippar, and Larsa. These fragments give similar accounts of the kings and their reigns and also mention events like the Great Flood. Some texts differ, presumably due to errors from the scribes who wrote the texts.

Pre-flood kings are said to have ruled for thousands of years. Eight specific kings are named before the Great Flood. Their reign totaled 241,200 years. Time in ancient Sumer was calculated in *sars*, which equaled 3,600 years; *ners*, which equaled 600 years; and *sosses*, which equaled 60 years.

The beginning of the Sumerian King List refers to a time when "kingship first descended from heaven" over 266,000 years before the civilization emerged. According to these clay fragments, Eridu was the first city on Earth.

Verifiable rulers who are mentioned in the Sumerian King List are Gilgamesh, Mesannepada, Enmebaragesi, Elulu, Meskiagnun, Enshakushanna, and Lugal-zage-si. These seven kings lend credibility to the Sumerian King List, although the order and timeframes differ vastly from the archaeological evidence that has been found. Egyptian dynastic information has even been used to correlate these dates.

The First King of Sumer: Alulim

If you are a believer that myths and legends have a grain of truth, then you should take a look at King Alulim. According to the Sumerian King List, Alulim was the first ruler of Sumer. Over eighteen Sumerian king lists have been found throughout the region, yet they all state that Alulim was the first king. No other information regarding King Alulim is found anywhere except for the Sumerian King List. The list states that the kingship descended from heaven and was established in Eridug (ancient Eridu) and that King Alulim ruled for 28,800 years.

Two notable historians have put forward their theories about King Alulim. The late professor of Assyrian and Babylonian literature at Yale University, William Wolfgang Hallo, posited that there is a link between King Alulim and the myth of Apkallu, the demi-god created by the god Enki who taught the ancient people of Sumer how to be cultured and civilized. Hallo also noted that Apkallu was an advisor to the early kings of Sumer and was described in cuneiform texts to be one of the fish-like men that lived before the Great Flood.

Archaeologist William H. Shea from the University of Michigan linked the name Alulim to Adapa, the son of the god Enki, and postulates that the name Adapa correlates with the name Adam, the first man according to the biblical narrative of Genesis. The Adam and Alulim theory is supported by many schools of thought today.

Great Kings of Ancient Sumer: Meshkiangasher and Enmerkar

King Meshkiangasher's name is included in the Sumerian King List, yet no archaeological evidence of his existence has been found in any other sources. In some versions of the Sumerian King List, this king is known as Meshkiangasher, but even then, he remains historically untraceable. In addition, the length of his reign is impossible. The myth surrounding King Meshkiangasher states that he ruled for 324 years and was the son of the sun god Utu. The myth states that at the time of his death, he descended toward the sea and ascended to the mountains. The ancient Sumerians believed this to be the path the sun followed across the sky and that this was a suitable time to travel since it was the path of the "son of the sun god."

Enmerkar, the heir of King Meshkiangasher became the first king of Uruk, which can be verified by archaeological evidence from numerous excavations. His kingship is recorded in the Sumerian King List. Issues arise when talking about the length of his rule. According to the Sumerian King List, it was over 420 years! The historical Enmerkar reigned at the end of the 4th millennium or the beginning of the 3rd millennium BCE.

Three epics about King Enmerkar have been discovered. "Enmerkar and the Lord of Aratta" is the longest epic that has been deciphered. This particular epic gives historians a great deal of cultural and religious information. It tells of King Enmerkar's jealousy of Aratta's immense wealth of stone and metal, which were used as building materials. King Enmerkar wanted to build a temple in Eridu dedicated to the god Enki, and he required special building materials. The goddess Inanna suggested that he send the lord of Aratta a threatening message and demand the building materials. The shrewd lord of Aratta was not afraid of the king and sent a message back demanding grain as payment for them.

King Enmerkar honored the lord's request, but the lord of Aratta reneged on the deal. The epic details many messages sent between the king and the lord, but unfortunately, the text is severely damaged. The conclusion of the epic appears to end in King Enmerkar's favor.

King Gilgamesh of Uruk

King Gilgamesh wrestling two bulls.
Osama Shukir Muhammed Amin FRCP(Glasg), CC BY-SA 4.0
https://creativecommons.org/licenses/by-sa/4.0 , via Wikimedia Commons;
https://commons.wikimedia.org/wiki/File:Gilgamesh_in_a_Sculptured_Vase,_Shara_Tem
ple,_Tell_Agrab,_Iraq.jpg

The period generally accepted by scholars for the reign of King Gilgamesh is between c. 2900 and 2350 BCE (the Early Dynastic period). According to the Sumerian King List, King Gilgamesh ruled for an impossible period of 126 years. Cuneiform texts state that Gilgamesh was the son of the priest-king Lugalbanda and the goddess Ninsun. Due to his demi-god heritage, Gilgamesh was blessed with superhuman strength and the perfect physique.

He was believed to be two-thirds god and one-third human, and the people revered him. This made him a fearful king who took what he wanted in wealth, women, and earthly possessions. His power and control were exaggerated, leading to the *Epic of Gilgamesh* and other myths and tales of wonder about his prowess as a king.

Later kings would claim him as their ancestor to gain power and respect from their subjects and kings of other regions. An example is King Shulgi of Ur, who claimed to be the brother of Gilgamesh and the son of Lugalbanda and the goddess Ninsun. Most historians consider Shulgi to have been the greatest ruler of the Ur III period.

The Infamous Female Monarch: Queen Kubaba

Kubaba, also known as Ku Bau or Kug-Baba, is the only female monarch on the Sumerian King List. What is interesting is that on the King List, she is named as the only ruler of the Third Dynasty of Kish. Textual evidence relates that she ruled around 2400 BCE for a period of one hundred years. Again, as with all the kings mentioned in the Sumerian King List, she is said to have ruled for over a century, which is not realistic. The Sumerian King List gives her the title of *lugal*, meaning "king," not *eresh*, meaning "queen consort." Kubaba is the only female in the history of Sumer to be given the title of *lugal*.

The legend of how Kubaba became queen is unusual. It appears that she was a beer brewer and tavern keeper in ancient Kish. In the ancient world, the brewing of beer was a respected profession since beer was a daily beverage enjoyed by the ancient Sumerians. Queen Kubaba must have been a successful and independent businesswoman.

Her legendary rise to the throne is detailed in the *Weidner Chronicle*, which states that the god Marduk saw Kubaba ask a fisherman to catch a fish and offer it at the temple dedicated to Marduk in Esagila. In return, she feeds the fisherman. When the god Marduk observes this act of veneration from Kubaba, he is so impressed by her devotion that he gives Kubaba the kingship of Sumer.

King Eannatum: The Conqueror

King Eannatum was the ruler of Lagash between c. 2500 and 2400 BCE. Lagash was a city-state that also ruled over Girsu, another city-state. Both these city-states were allocated fertile lands in Gu-Edin or Guedena. To the north lay Umma, another city-state that also farmed fertile lands in Guedena. This caused adversity between the city-states, especially since Lagash and Girsu assisted each other in the form of loans when supplies were needed.

A treaty established by Mesilim, King of Kish, during the Third Dynasty kept Lagash and Girsu from warfare with Umma. This treaty was inscribed on a pillar that was placed in Guedena.

King Eannatum did not immediately break this treaty once he started conquering regions. He had a well-devised plan of action to establish an empire. He started by invading Elam, east of Sumer, in today's Iran. Elam had access to tin, which was used to make bronze. Additionally, Elam had an established trade network that brought wealth to the area.

The next city-state conquered was Urua in the fertile region of Susiana. With these two victories, Eannatum was confident enough to invade Umma. After his victory in Umma, King Eannatum had control over the fertile Guedena, access to additional soldiers, materials for weaponry, and the ambition to further expand his kingdom.

An interesting fact to note about King Eannatum is that neither his father, King Akurgal, nor his grandfather, Ur-Nanshe, appear on the Sumerian King List. King Eannatum is the first historically verifiable king of Sumer.

Warfare in Ancient Sumer

The need for fertile land and a sufficient supply of water for farming, as well as drinking water for animals and humans, created constant conflicts between city-states.

As city-states grew and increased in population, the need for land, water, and other resources led to the development of weapons, technology, strategy, and armies for conquering neighboring city-states and surrounding regions.

The first verifiable archaeological evidence detailing a serious, strategic war was when King Eannatum of Lagash conquered the city-state of Umma in c. 2525 BCE. The famous Stele of the

Vultures, housed in the Louvre, depicts vultures and lions ripping flesh from corpses on a desert plain.

The victorious King Eannatum was a master of propaganda and commanded the creation of this pictorial stele that showed him leading warriors in a chariot drawn by donkeys. This stele shows that the Sumerians fought in a phalanx formation and that warriors had body armor, copper helmets, spears, and axes. King Eannatum was struck in the eye with an arrow in the battle, which only made him more determined to win and conquer more city-states.

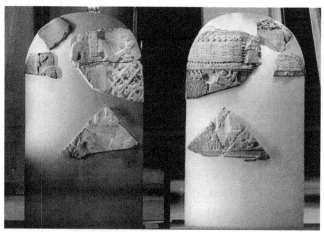

Stele of the Vultures, front and back view.
Background: Kikuyu3Elements: Eric Gaba (User: Sting) Composite: पाटलिपुत्र (talk) 10:52, 30 April 2020 (UTC), CC BY-SA 4.0 https://creativecommons.org/licenses/by-sa/4.0 ,via Wikimedia Commons;https://commons.wikimedia.org/wiki/File:Stele_of_the_Vultures_in_the_Louvre_Museum _(enhanced_composite).jpg

The strategies used in this battle are well detailed on the stele and many clay tablets that talk about the victories of King Eannatum. Fighting in a phalanx formation requires training, discipline, and planning—and all of this is attributed to King Eannatum.

The technological advancement of bronze helmets denotes the development of the first defensive response in warfare. It made the mace, a weapon with a pole and a stone head, an inferior weapon on the battlefield.

King Eannatum led his army onto the battlefield in a wheeled chariot; this is considered to be a major technological innovation in warfare. Although it is referred to as a chariot, it is more accurate to call it a "battle car" since it lacked maneuverability and speed.

The Sumerians are also believed to have invented the rein-ring to better control donkeys and an axle in front of the chariot platform. This axle, in all probability, would not have been used during battles since it increased the chariot's weight and decreased stability when traveling at faster speeds.

Later developments in weaponry were javelins and axes. Bows and arrows were notably absent during these battles. Scholars posit that the sight of an opponent riding a chariot in front of the phalanx formation would scare the enemy away.

Unification of the City-States

King Etana of Kish is said to have united many of the city-states for the first time. After his death in c. 2800 BCE, these city-states broke apart again. They began to challenge and conquer each other, and the previously unified Sumer became a target for other regions, such as the Elamites and the later Akkadians.

Chapter 9 – Culture and Innovation

The ancient Sumerian inventions are a testament to what the human mind is capable of in extreme and adverse conditions. The mind's ability to form original thoughts and ideas is illustrated uniquely by the Sumerian civilization. They invented systems, tools, equipment, and methods to deal with all aspects of individual and communal daily life. They adapted their lifestyles and culture to thrive in the environment in which they lived.

Inventions like the wheel, something we cannot live without today, were invented by the Sumerians. Other amazing inventions that we still use today include cosmetic sets, harps, hammers, axes, weapons, the plow, the sailboat, and a written language, among other things.

The Earliest Form of Writing

Cuneiform is believed to be the earliest form of writing. It was invented as a way to keep track of transactions, storage, and administration matters; in other words, it was an ancient form of bookkeeping. It developed from simple drawings into stylized pictographs and then into logosyllabic writing, which could be used to express concepts and thoughts.

The first discovery of cuneiform was at the archaeological site of Jemdet Nasr. This settlement dated back to the Ubaid period and lasted into the Early Dynastic period. These tablets from Jemdet Nasr are dated to the second half of the 4th millennium BCE. The script is in the proto-cuneiform or Archaic style. Proto-cuneiform is a complex script, and scholars posit that it includes both numerical and non-numerical signs. The writings on the earliest tablets have not been deciphered yet, but it is assumed to be Sumerian.

As time passed, the script developed into the iconic wedge-shaped appearance that we now associate with cuneiform. Archives in Uruk and other excavated sites have contemporary tablets of the same proto script developing into true cuneiform, changing first into a mixture and then into logosyllabic signs.

The tablets are primarily administrative, detailing lists of animals, objects, and food that were distributed to the inhabitants, suggesting a centralized authority in charge of distribution. Clay tablets have complex calculations of the exact size of agricultural fields, which is the earliest record of this type of calculation. Other texts calculate beer, grain, and fruit distribution to traders and laborers, while other texts have a detailed accounting system for livestock.

Around 2400 BCE, cuneiform was adapted to write the Akkadian language, and it was later adapted for the Assyrian and Babylonian languages. These are Semitic languages and form the basis of today's Hebrew and Arabic scripts. Cuneiform was taken over and adapted over time to write almost all of the languages of the ancient Near East. Akkadian became the lingua franca, except, of course, for the ancient Egyptian language. But even Egyptian scribes knew cuneiform. International diplomatic correspondence discovered at the archives of Tell el-Amarna from the time of Pharaoh Akhenaten and Queen Nefertiti (c. 14th century BCE) contained a host of cuneiform letters from several ancient Near East nations.

The Sumerian language and the cuneiform script were known to scribes until the 1ˢᵗ century CE. Sumerian lexicons and literature with translations into other ancient Near East languages were part of scribal training. It is partly thanks to these lexicons that scholars were able to confirm the existence of the Sumerians. Modern translations of Sumerian literature in the form of myths, legends, temple hymns, and poems are mostly from these ancient scribal copies that have been found in archives across the ancient Near East.

Agricultural Innovations

The land between the lower Tigris and Euphrates Rivers was fertile because the seasonal floods deposited silt across the alluvial plains. Rainfall was scarce, so the Sumerians had either too much or too little water available for crop production. They had to come up with innovative ideas to water their crops and, at the same time, protect settlements and crops from destruction by the occasionally severe floods.

The Sumerians developed drainage and irrigation systems to ensure consistent water supplies for crops, people, and livestock throughout the year. Ancient farmers used existing natural levees created by the flooding rivers to control the water. They built new earthern levees and dikes along riverbanks to control the water during flooding. When the fields were dry, the ancient Sumerians made holes in the levees to let the water flow between the fields. Ditches were cut into the fields to carry water to the crops. The Sumerians also conserved water by building dams and reservoirs, from which canals carried water to cities and fields.

The construction of canals was not limited to agricultural use. Canals were built to divert floodwaters away from the villages and cities. These same canals could then be used to irrigate the lands during dry periods. Canals were also built to redirect water from the rivers farther inland to cultivate more crops. The larger canals were used as waterways for transporting trade goods and food.

Ancient engineers devised irrigation systems that varied in depth and design depending on the natural geography of the area. Large canals were built directly out of the rivers. They diverged into smaller canals and then into even smaller furrows or ditches that flowed directly into the fields.

The ancient Sumerians had an intricate irrigation system, and at times, aqueducts and raised canals were built to accommodate topographical issues. Further advances in the irrigation systems included mechanisms like the shaduf (shadoof), which was a pivoted pole with a bucket at one end and a weight at the other. The shaduf was used to lift water from rivers, dams, or canals onto the fields. Later, the Sumerians developed a noria. This was a wheeled device with buckets attached at the rim that moved water to irrigate lands.

Sumerians not only developed these intricate irrigation systems but also implemented administrative structures that scheduled dredging, repairs, and maintenance of these systems. This was of major importance since it ensured smooth operation and the fair distribution of water. The building of irrigation systems, their overall administration, and their scheduled maintenance were recorded on cuneiform tablets.

Clogging and silting of canals and waterways was a constant problem, especially with water from the slower moving and shallower Euphrates River that carried and deposited large amounts of silt. The heavy silt of the Euphrates contained considerable amounts of minerals, including salt. Archaeologists and other scholars of ancient history are convinced that the deep and heavy silt that covers the area today still hides many secrets yet to be discovered.

By using these innovative irrigation systems, the Sumerians successfully cultivated barley, wheat, dates, onions, cucumbers, apples, and a variety of herbs and spices.

Tools Used for Agriculture

Initially, animal horns and sticks were used to make furrows in the soil, and the seeds were sown and watered by hand. This was labor-intensive and fetched limited results. As the population increased, the Sumerians realized they had to find a way to cultivate more land to yield a bigger harvest.

Archaeologists have discovered evidence of the first plow dating back to at least the early 4th millennium BCE. The Sumerians developed a seeder plow during the beginning of the Early Dynastic period. The seeder plow enabled farmers to use oxen to till the soil and plant the seeds simultaneously. These innovations boosted harvests tremendously and provided surplus grain for export.

Sumerian Farmer's Almanac

This clay tablet containing 111 lines of cuneiform text was discovered at the Nippur site. It is a set of instructions from a father to his son detailing how the land should be prepared and at what time of the year the processes of crop planting should be undertaken. Provisions should be made for an extra ox to pull the plow—yet further evidence that the plow was in use by that time. The instruction manual also provides information on when and how to harvest.

The Invention of the Calendar

The Sumerian lunar calendar may have been invented for religious purposes and agricultural activities. The calendar allowed the Sumerians to determine which phase of agriculture they should be focusing on. It gave the Sumerians advance knowledge of the seasons and impending floods so that they could make the necessary preparations.

The lunar calendar functioned well for short periods, but the Sumerians soon realized that it was inadequate for longer periods. Their lunar calendar had a year of 354 days over twelve months, which the Sumerians rounded up to 360 days.

The Sumerian Lunisolar Calendar

By the end of the Early Dynastic period, Sumerian mathematicians, astronomers, priests, and scribes had devised a lunisolar calendar. This meant the calendar was now synchronized across the three natural cycles:

1. Day and night were divided into two twelve-hour periods

2. The lunar month was based on the monthly cycles of the moon, and a week could be based on each phase of the monthly cycle.

3. The solar cycle worked according to the changes in the sun's elevation above the horizon throughout one year.

The Sumerians calculated twelve lunar months for a year, and it took around 354.36 days to complete the cycle of a lunar year. This did not match up with the cycles of the sun. The ancient Sumerians calculated these differences and accounted for them by adding an extra month every two to three years. This was eventually done by royal decree since they were not yet measuring the precise alignments of the lunar and solar years at that time, at least as far as we know. The later Babylonians were the first to math these differences more precisely.

It is generally accepted that months, weeks, and days were first used during the Ur III period, and there are documents detailing that four weeks made up a month. The months were divided into two halves, which were based on the waxing and waning cycles of the moon.

Although the Sumerians did not calculate the calendar exactly, it is still a magnificent feat of astronomy and mathematics.

Development of a Sumerian Legal System

When humans live together in a society, there is a need for rules and regulations. As a fully developed civilization, the Sumerians naturally had laws, even before recorded history. The laws may not have been the same in each city-state, but it can be assumed that they were similar because the culture, language, and lifestyles were similar.

It was once thought that the law codes inscribed by King Hammurabi of Babylon (c. 1792–1750 BCE) were the first written laws. This is incorrect; Sumerian King Ur-Nammu had laws inscribed around 2100 BCE.

The earliest known law code was called the Code of Urukagina. He was the last king of the city-state of Lagash in the 24th century BCE. There are no extant copies of this pre-Akkadian legal code; knowledge of it only survives through references in other writings. It is said that Urukagina's law code protected widows, orphans, and the poor through tax exemptions.

The Law Code of Ur-Nammu

Tablet containing two fragments excavated in Nippur dating back to c. 2150–2050 BCE.
Istanbul Archaeology Museums, CC0, via Wikimedia Commons;
https://commons.wikimedia.org/wiki/File:Ur_Nammu_code_Istanbul.jpg

The first text of the oldest preserved law code, the Code of Ur-Nammu, was found in Nippur. The code found in Nippur was incomplete, but later copies found at Ur enabled scholars to reconstruct most of it. It was very much an "eye-for-an-eye" kind of legal code for serious crimes, although scholars were surprised to find that many bodily crimes sometimes carried fines rather than physical punishment. An exception would be the law for a son striking his father; he was punished by having his hand chopped off. The code dealt with public and civil matters as well.

Many scholars think the laws should be attributed to King Ur-Nammu's son, Shulgi, because it seems they were distributed widely and displayed publicly during his reign.

Sumerian Housing

Social stratification seems to have been firmly entrenched by the Early Dynastic period. By that time, the early model of extended families sharing the burden of agricultural labor had long been replaced by external aid and increasing technological advances. The natural outcome of vast food production freed hands for the development of other industries, and the labor requirements could be met for monumental building projects.

The Sumerians from the Ubaid period lived in tripartite houses. This floor plan was used as the base for all buildings. As their society, culture, and religion progressed, they began to build more elaborate structures, such as temples, ziggurats, and magnificent palaces. Later upper-class houses were sometimes multi-storied. These houses still used the tripartite floor plan from the early Ubaid period.

The first city walls were built for protection against flooding. They were later built for defensive purposes. These walls also had a social element. Where one's house was located inside the city walls would indicate one's status in society. Houses were built in the suburbs, and the closer to the ziggurat a house was, the higher one's status in society was. Officials, priests, and the elites lived in the suburbs, while traders, shopkeepers, and fishermen lived on the outskirts of the city and sometimes outside the city walls.

Music

Ancient Sumerian musical instruments were found as grave goods during archaeological excavations. Musicians and their instruments are depicted in artworks. There were string, wind, and percussion instruments.

Musicians in Mesopotamia were well trained and a recognized professional class. The Sumerians must have found the music to be soothing when instruments like lyres and flutes made from bone or reeds were used. There were also discoveries of hand-held drums and rattles. We know the Sumerians loved to sing, as can be seen with the lamentations. In some of the festival halls where plates and beer jugs were excavated, musical instruments were also found.

Cylinder seal found in the tomb inscribed as Pu-A-Bi- Nin (Queen Puabi), showing her attendants playing the lyre.
Nic McPhee from Morris, Minnesota, USA, CC BY-SA 2.0
https://creativecommons.org/licenses/by-sa/2.0 , via Wikimedia Commons;
https://commons.wikimedia.org/wiki/File:Flickr_-_Nic%27s_events_-
_British_Museum_with_Cory_and_Mary,_6_Sep_2007_-_185.jpg

Musical instruments were found in the burial sites of the elites, such as in the grave of the "Lady of Puabi," also referred to as the "Queen of Puabi." This tomb was found in the royal cemetery of Ur. Her grave was given elite status, and it was posited that she may have ruled separately and without a husband. Her grave goods were utterly magnificent.

The bull's head from the lyre found in the tomb of Queen Puabi.
Osama Shukir Muhammed Amin FRCP(Glasg), CC BY-SA 4.0
https://creativecommons.org/licenses/by-sa/4.0 via Wikimedia Commons;
https://commons.wikimedia.org/wiki/File:Bull%27s_head_of_the_Queen%27s_lyre_from_Pu-
abi%27s_grave_PG_800,_the_Royal_Cemetery_at_Ur,_Southern_Mesopotamia,_Iraq._The_Britis
h_Museum,_London.JPG

Art and Crafts

Sumerian arts and crafts were limited by the natural elements found in their geographical region. They resorted to clay or fired clay to produce pottery, plates, and statues. In comparison, the Greeks would use marble, which was readily available, to produce massive statues.

Sumerian Art

Massive sculptures of the patron deity of each city-state have been discovered; some are even life-sized! These statues were magnificent in proportion and decorated in an effort to curry favor with the gods. They had inlays of shells, precious stones, and colorful mosaics in geometrical patterns. Depictions on clay and stone have been found showing fighting or hunting, telling us a substantial amount about the daily lives of Sumerian men.

Crafts

Intricate chairs were handcrafted using wood and reeds, and they were inlaid with shells and mosaics. Archaeologists have excavated beautiful pottery, statues, and portraits of animals created from mosaics and shells. The pottery of the ancient Sumerians was so beautiful that it was used to pay for goods traded with neighboring city-states.

Sumerian jewelry was magnificent. Craftspeople inlaid gold with lapis lazuli and other precious stones for the elite, as indicated by grave goods. Poor people also wore jewelry, but it was crafted from shells, wood, seeds, and bones.

Reconstructed Sumerian headgear and necklaces found in the tomb of Puabi. This set was found on three of her attendants, and this reconstruction is housed at the British Museum.

Other intricate crafts include the inlaid helmets used by soldiers, cylinder seals, and decorated tables.

Sumerian Cloth

Sumerian clothing was made of flax or wool. Women were responsible for weaving. Weaving was an essential skill, and the Sumerians excelled at it. Reeds were abundant in the marshlands and on the riverbanks. Fresh reeds are pliable, which enabled the Sumerians to use them in multiple ways.

For instance, ancient Sumerians wore sandals made from woven reeds. They also made extremely durable baskets. These baskets were strong enough to haul clay for mudbricks from the river to the manufacturing site. Reed baskets were also used to carry grain.

Large woven baskets were put on the backs of pack animals, such as donkeys. Evidence suggests that Sumerian baskets were of excellent quality. They were exported and have been found at sites across the region. Records have been found of exported Sumerian cloth at several ancient Near Eastern sites as well.

Reed baskets that were waterproofed with bitumen were used to carry water. Bitumen-treated reeds were used to close off canals, much in the same way that we use a sluice gate today.

Houses and other buildings had woven mats from reeds that were lined with bitumen. They formed the foundations and protected the mudbricks.

Daily Life

There were times when life for all the people of ancient Sumer was comfortable and safe. They all had houses, enough food, and time for recreation. But times change. As the civilization matured, it lost its innocence. Personal wealth and power created social stratification, and greed and envy replaced an attitude of sharing.

Daily life in Sumer was hard for the workers; a workday was thought to be ten hours long. Professions included teaching, building, and farming for men, while women typically stayed home and looked after the chores at home and raised children. Wealthy families could employ tutors to homeschool their children.

The people enjoyed recreational activities, such as boxing, racing, wrestling, hunting, storytelling, dancing, and music. This is attested by some of the more than 120,000 clay tablets found at the Ashurbanipal library that was excavated in Nineveh and other major archaeological sites, such as Ur, Uruk, Nippur, and Larsa.

School

Schools were run by priests. Priests beat the boys if they did not do well at school since it was believed that a lesson could only be reinforced by a good beating; therefore, only boys were allowed to attend school. However, since most Sumerians were thought to be illiterate, it is likely only boys from the upper classes and those seeking certain positions to advance in society went to school. Typically, only girls from elite classes could have a formal education. Her parents would employ a tutor so she could learn at home.

Games and Toys

The ancient Sumerians were hard workers yet understood there must be a balance between work and home life. They made toys for their children to play with, such as spinning tops, slingshots, balls, jump ropes, rattles, and hoops. According to some sources, the girls had toys resembling dollhouses, complete with miniature furniture. Children even had miniature carts and chariots that were pulled with strings or ropes and miniature boats that floated.

Board Games

The board game found at the royal burial grounds in Ur is intricate. The board dates back to the 3rd millennium BCE and indicates that two opposing players would use strategy, time, and luck to beat the other player, much like a game of chess. Evidence of this game was found across Sumer and Mesopotamia and as far as Crete and Sri Lanka.

Sumerians invented other board games, one of which is referred to as twenty squares or fifty-eight holes. Pieces on the board were moved into the holes, but the rules and objectives of the game have not yet been discovered. Other games used dice, and some games were associated with gambling. Board games were played by all social classes.

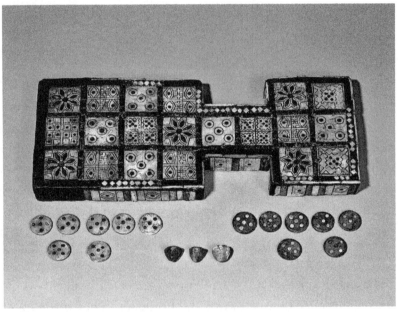

Sumerians are credited with the invention of the board game.
British Museum, CC BY-SA 4.0 https://creativecommons.org/licenses/by-sa/4.0 via Wikimedia Commons; https://commons.wikimedia.org/wiki/File:Royal_Game_of_Ur_03.jpg

Button Buzz

The Sumerians played a game called button buzz. To start, one needed a circle made of clay. A string or rope was tied to this circular disc. The aim of the game was to swing the disc by a piece of rope or weed as fast as possible. Once it went fast enough, it made a buzzing sound. The winner would be the person whose clay disc made the loudest sound.

Technological Advancements

There is no doubt that the Sumerians were very innovative people. When faced with a problem, they simply found a way to overcome the challenge, whether that was to sail across the water, irrigate the fields, defend themselves, or work out time and mathematical equations. They did it all. The most amazing thing is that they did it all without any assistance or prior knowledge.

Mathematics, Arithmetic, Geometry, and Astronomy

In ancient Sumer, the people soon learned that if they were going to trade with each other and other city-states, they had to develop a system that allowed them to count, take measurements of land, and pay laborers wages. Tablets dating back to 2500 BCE have detailed land measurements, accounting, and records of taxation.

Long-form division, multiplication, geometric, and algebraic calculations have been deciphered from clay tablets dating back to 2600 BCE. In addition to these calculations, tablets using mathematics were also found that depicted sky charts for navigational purposes and a detailed lunar calendar, as well as the first zodiac, which was divided into twelve sections.

Numerical System

The Sumerians created a sexagesimal numerical system. This means all calculations were worked out using the number sixty as the base number. This was already in effect in the 3rd millennium BCE. The Sumerians further progressed this numerical system into sixty seconds and sixty minutes, which became an hour. They were also the first to create the 360° circle. The first abacus was also a Sumerian invention.

Astrology

Ancient Sumerians had a polytheistic religion and worshiped a large number of human-like gods and goddesses. These deities were believed to control the sun, moon, and planets, as well as natural occurrences like wind and rain. Ancient Sumerian astronomers discovered that planets and stars moved in specific patterns around the sun and moon. To them, it seemed as if the gods were sending coded messages that they had to interpret. This was how their belief in astrology developed.

The Sumerians used their mathematical calculations to determine the cycles of the sun, moon, planets, and stars to determine things like as full moons, half moons, and the waxing and waning phases of the moon. They also calculated and predicted eclipses.

Sumerian Boats

The invention of the boat is credited to the Sumerians, as they used the Tigris and the Euphrates as trade routes. The city-state of Ur was also located on the shores of the Persian Gulf at that time. Boats were made out of reeds that were bound together and covered with animal hides. The first examples of reed-bundle boats were ceramic models of them; these were found at sites like Eridu, Uruk, and Tell el-'Oueili. The details on the ceramic models are so clear that it shows incisions, mimicking the reeds that would have been used to construct a real boat. Another example depicts a reed boat with masts and sails. Additionally, excavated pieces of reed with bitumen and barnacles have been discovered. These are pieces of an actual boat, which would make it the earliest seafaring vessel in the world.

Mesopotamian reed boats are dated back to around 5500 BCE, which is the early Neolithic Ubaid period. Ubaid ships were made from reed bundles bound together by rope and then waterproofed with bitumen. In addition, these boats often had long poles to push them down the river. Some had masts for sails. The sails would have been made from linen or flax. Ropes were used to hoist the sails up to the top of the masts. Some discoveries indicate that these reed boats had upturned bows to protect them from oncoming waves of water.

Bronze

Evidence shows that smelting copper started as early as 6000 BCE in Sumer. Archaeologists dated the making of bronze, which is made by smelting tin and copper together, to c. 3500 BCE.

The use of copper was one of the Sumerians' major innovations, and cities like Ur, Uruk, and Tell al-'Ubaid show that they made tools, such as arrowheads, harpoons, chisels, and axes, from copper and later progressed to bronze. Bronze was harder and made weapons more deadly. Copper was used for personal items like razors, jugs, and elaborate drinking vessels.

This lion-headed eagle (Imdugud or Anzu), the symbol of the god Ningirsu. The eagle grasps two deer, one on either side. This panel was found at the base of the temple of Ninhursag at Tell al-'Ubaid. It is made from copper and dates to around 3100 BCE.
Vassil, CC0, via Wikimedia Commons;
https://commons.wikimedia.org/wiki/File:British_Museum_Middle_east_14022019_Panel_Imdugud_2500_BC_3640.jpg

Weapons

The Bronze Age gave rise to stronger weapons. City-states were able to fight and invade other city-states with greater confidence due to this new harder alloy. Bronze knives, lance points, and arrowheads made weapons more durable and deadlier in battles.

The First Form of Identification

Ancient Sumerians kept written records of all their transactions, but most of them did not know how to read and write cuneiform. Sumerians who did not know how to read or write would commission a cylinder seal with unique pictograms—like a signature. This form of identification was not only for people who could not read or write. It was the preferred method of marking messages, trade goods, or any other property. Thousands of these cylinder seals have been excavated. Many of them belong to the working class, although more elaborate ones were used by the upper class.

Sumerian Seals

Stamp seals date back to 5000 BCE. These objects have simple markings to denote the number of goods sold. Archaeologists found seals on storeroom doors, baskets, and bags. In around 3500 BCE, stamp seals progressed to cylinder seals, which could be rolled over wet clay, leaving a permanent marking.

Cylinder seal of Adda.
Nic McPhee from Morris, Minnesota, USA, CC BY-SA 2.0
https://creativecommons.org/licenses/by-sa/2.0 via Wikimedia Commons;
https://commons.wikimedia.org/wiki/File:Adda_Seal_Akkadian_Empire_2300_BC.jpg

Beer-making Process

It was assumed that another interesting first for the Sumerians was the brewing of beer until the discovery of beer residue in vessels from Göbekli Tepe. It is thought beer was made at the site thousands of years before the Sumerians brewed beer. Nevertheless, evidence of a Sumerian beer recipe was found in a poem dedicated to Ninkasi dating to c. 3900 BCE. This poem dedicated to the tutelage of the goddess of beer also shows the important role women played in society since they were the primary brewers in ancient Sumer.

Archaeological evidence of Sumerian beer dates back to 3500 BCE, as chemical traces of beer were found in excavated jars. Depictions of drinking beer show that it was done using straws due to the thick consistency of the liquid. Drinking beer in this way would have prevented the people from gulping down the bitter solids left over from fermentation.

Chapter 10 – Myths and Religion

Sumerian religion was as complex as the origin of its people. Ancient texts that have been deciphered tell us that each Sumerian city had a primary deity. Although humans and gods lived together, humans were only there to serve and worship the gods.

The Sumerian pantheon had hundreds of gods and goddesses and even some demons. The Sumerian deities were all related, and they were remarkably human in their behavior. They acted out of pity, kindness, rage, jealousy, betrayal, spite, and all the other emotions that humans are capable of—the good and the bad.

The main pantheon of deities were sons and mothers, sisters and brothers, or fathers and daughters that intermarried. The sun, moon, planets, animals, and plants manifested as gods and goddesses.

Scribes used clay tablets to tell stories that were once orally transmitted from generation to generation in each tribe. The archaeological discoveries of lengthy clay cuneiform tablets filled with myths and legends are considered to be the oldest myths in the world. They give scholars an understanding of the Sumerians' ideology and beliefs.

Accordingly, it was believed the deities were responsible for all things that happened in the celestial and human world.

The Development of the Pantheon

The Sumerians believed that the Earth was flat and enclosed in a dome that formed the heavens above and the underworld beneath. This was the universe over which the deities ruled. They would bless the humans with good harvests or alternately punishments if the humans were displeasing them.

Cuneiform tablets dating to the 3rd millennium BCE attribute the creation of the world to four primary deities: Enlil, Enki, Ninhursag, and An. These deities presided over daily occurrences, such as disease, health, crops, and floods. They determined wealth, poverty, and other human experiences. Generally, these gods were seen as helpful to humans, but they could be whimsical, mischievous, and malevolent. This was how the people explained events and catastrophes like earthquakes and floods.

Enlil – The Air God

Enlil, the air god, was the most important deity to the Sumerians. His breath could bring gentle winds or hurricanes, and he was the manifestation of energy, authority, and force. He was also the god of agriculture, and the people depended on him for their livelihood and wealth. One of the myths surrounding Enlil says that he was banished to the underworld after he raped his consort, Ninlil, the grain goddess. This myth was developed to explain the agricultural cycles: the fertilization of the land, ripening of the crops, harvesting, and then inactivity during the winter months.

An – Father of the Gods

An, also referred to as Anu, was the head of the Sumerian pantheon and seen as the father of the gods, the supreme ruler who maintained the entire existence of the heavens and the Earth. An is often featured in the background of myths; he was rarely the central figure.

One of the main centers of worship was Uruk, which was at times referred to as "the city of Anu." An was the father of the god Enlil and is depicted as a human wearing a horned headdress or a bull with a human head. As the primary god, An gave commands to the other gods and goddesses. In later myths, he ceded his power to his son Enlil and became more remote.

Enki – God of Wisdom and Magic

In the beginning, Earth was surrounded by an ancient saltwater sea. Fresh water came from underneath the Earth from an underworld sea called the Abzu. Enki lived in the Abzu and was known for being mischievous. According to ancient Sumerian texts, Enki was virile and embodied masculinity. His depictions often include sexual representations, particularly the life-giving characteristics of the god's semen and the fresh waters of the Abzu for agricultural purposes. In art, he is shown as a bearded, robe-wearing god with a horned cap.

Enki's sexual exploits include various goddesses, such as his daughter, Ninmu, and his granddaughter by Ninmu named Ninkurra. Enki was a son of An and had the power of wisdom, magic, and incantations. He is often linked to the city of Eridu. Beliefs surrounding Enki include exorcism. Disease and strife were believed to be the result of demonic possession or displeasing divine powers. As such, incantations were used to remove the evil presence from occupying people or places.

Depiction of the god Enki.
https://commons.wikimedia.org/wiki/File:Copia_de_Enki.jpg

Ninhursag – Mother Goddess

Ninhursag, known as the mother goddess, is one of the four creation deities. Evidence of a goddess figurine suggests she was worshiped during the Ubaid period around 4,500 BCE. Her name means "Lady of the Sacred Mountain." As one of the creator deities, Ninhursag is the goddess of fertility, childbirth, and growth. She is also called the mother of the Earth. Ninhursag was asked to bless unborn children and to ensure food after a child's birth.

She was the patron deity of Adab, a prominent Sumerian city-state. As the mother of the gods and the mother of men, Ninhursag is the most important female deity. All the myths of Ninhursag state that she had power over life and death. In the myth of Enki and Ninhursag, she can draw out or remove diseases and heal sickness.

Depictions of the mother goddess often show her seated in front of a mountain wearing a layered skirt, either with her hair in the style of the Greek omega symbol or with a horned headdress. Some depictions of her include ibex, deer, bison, and eagles.

The Entemena vase motif depicting Ninhursag as a stag with lions greeting her in a friendly manner.
https://commons.wikimedia.org/wiki/File:Entemena_vase_motif.jpg

Worship and Festivities

Temples in each city-state were dedicated to its patron god or goddess. At the temples, the deities were worshiped and besieged for blessings.

Priests and priestesses lived in the temples, which allowed them to be available for daily rituals and worship. They were the only ones allowed in the ziggurats. Castraters (a person who performs castration ceremonies) and temple slaves lived in separate buildings close to the temple.

The people were expected to pray daily or bring sacrifices to the priests. These sacrifices could be votive statues or food, which the priests placed on and around the temple altar.

Temples were a central feature in the lives of the public. Singing and music were a part of daily worship, as was the consumption of beer and wine. There were also annual and monthly feasts.

Sumerians made private worship a part of their lives. Each Sumerian had a personal or family god, and they would go to the temple to wail, plead, and lament while confessing their daily sins and pleading for mercy. They would beg their family god to intervene on their behalf.

The mother goddess was venerated in festivities by ten vocalists, ten instrumentalists, and sixty-two lamentation priests during rituals in Lagash. In general, festivities included music, dancing, drinking barley beer, and eating meat and vegetables. This is evident at all the temple sites, as archaeologists have uncovered plates, cups, and vases with traces of barley beer, as well as large ovens. Great quantities of meat were cooked and consumed, as can be seen from the animal bones found at these sites.

The main festival halls contained many hearths, which confirms that festivities were held year-round, including during the cold winter months.

Annual Festivals

Dumuzi - This Sumerian festival celebrated the god Dumuzi, the god of life and death. The festivities were meant to bring Dumuzi back from the underworld to join with the goddess of life, Inanna. These celebrations were held during winter times to explain why crops and fields died during the cold.

Inanna Feast - This feast focused on the initial descent of the goddess Inanna to the underworld, where she was held captive by the goddess of death and rebirth, Ereshkigal. Inanna was a prisoner in the underworld until she agreed to call upon Dumuzi to stay in the underworld during winter.

Marriage to the Goddess - This was believed to be the most important festival in ancient Sumer. It was celebrated annually and celebrated when Dumuzi married Inanna. The current king would represent Dumuzi, and a priestess of the temple would represent Inanna. These festivities always took place around New Year's and were thought to bring prosperity to the king and all of Sumer for the year.

The Akitu Festival - During the Late Uruk period, this ritual festival had two processions: one going to the Akitu House and one returning. The processions were dedicated to the gods An and

Inanna. They are described as opulent and richly decorated, and the festivities lasted for seven days. Historians posit that the festival of Akitu probably originated in Ur during the equinox since it coincided with the emergence of the moon god Nanna, which was symbolized by the waxing of the moon. During the Akitu festival in Ur, a statue of the moon god Nanna was brought into the city via a barge from the Akitu House, which was located outside the city. When other city-states adopted this festival, it was changed to revere the god or goddess of that city-state. These reenactments would occur at different times of the year to ensure they did not happen on a conflicting date with the festival of the chief moon god Nanna. This festival was the main event on Nippur's calendar, which was the religious center of the Sumerians.

Worship at the Temple of Enlil

The temple of Enlil, excavated in Dur-Kurigalzu, was a religious site where offerings of votive statues, rituals accompanied by music, and singing would be performed for the god Enlil in return for blessings. Enlil was the god of winds, storms, air, and earth, and it was believed he ensured that crops were nourished sufficiently and produced a good yield.

Temples Dedicated to the Deities

Before the first kings, the city leaders ruled in the form of a council of elders. Their duty was to ensure the patron god or goddess and the gods in general were pleased with the people's sacrifices, ceremonies, and rituals. If the gods were pleased, they would bless the people. Their health would be good, and they would be free of accidents and disease.

Temple architecture was the same throughout Sumer. The *cella*, a long central hall, ended in an altar dedicated to the god or goddess of the temple. Behind the altar was an alcove, where a statue representing the deity was placed. Small rooms used by the priests and priestesses for sleeping were built on the sides of the rectangular building. Temples were magnificently decorated with geometric mosaics and frescoes depicting animals and humans.

The White Temple – Dedicated to the God An

The father of the gods, An, was revered at the White Temple in Uruk. Uruk was a major city-state during the 4th millennium BCE and the chief god of the city. This spectacular temple was painted white and had four corners oriented in the cardinal directions.

The Temple Dedicated to the God Enki

Enki was the main deity of Eridu. Archaeological excavations at this site have found evidence dating back to the early Ubaid period, around 6500 BCE. Evidence shows that this temple was reconstructed and expanded at least eighteen times. The shrine dedicated to the god Enki had a water pool located at the main entrance. In the pool area, archaeologists have uncovered the bones of carp fish, leading to the idea that feasts were held in the temple itself. The temple was abandoned during the Persian invasion.

Temples Dedicated to the Mother Goddess, Ninhursag

Since Ninhursag was considered the mother goddess, temples were dedicated to her in many of the city-states. Before the people recognized Ninhursag as the mother goddess, some scholars posit that she was worshiped as a goddess across the region and, therefore, did not have a major temple associated with one specific city.

Temples dedicated to Ninhursag were excavated in Nippur that dated to the Ur III period. In Adab, Babylon, and Girsu, she was venerated under the regional names of Diĝirmah, Ninmah, and E-mah, respectively.

The Early Dynastic temple at Ur is dedicated to the goddess Ninhursag. It has an inscription on the temple that reads, "Aanepada King of Ur, Son of Mesanepada King of Ur, has built this for his lady Ninhursag."

Gilgamesh and the Netherworld

Gilgamesh is the well-known hero and king of ancient Mesopotamia. The collection of tablets that detail his exploits has collectively been named "the odyssey of the king who did not want to die."

Twelve clay tablets written in Akkadian at the library in Nineveh detail King Gilgamesh's quest for immortality. Also discovered at the library were five other poems with myths about the hero-king Gilgamesh. These poems had titles describing his fight with the Bull of Heaven, his death, his exploits of the netherworld, and more.

Gilgamesh was the king of Uruk. He was the first king to build a defensive wall around his city-state. King Gilgamesh wanted Uruk to be seen as powerful and wealthy, and he commanded the construction of temple towers and magnificent ziggurats. He was personally involved in the planning and layout of agricultural lands and orchards. He was known for his beautiful physique, strength, and intelligence, which makes sense since the people believed him to be two-thirds god and one-third human.

At the start of his rule, Gilgamesh was cruel and lorded over his subjects. He raped women from any class of society; it did not matter whether she was noble, a warrior's wife, or a peasant. He used slave labor and worked his slaves to the point of exhaustion.

When the gods learn of Gilgamesh's exploits and as the people cried, wailed, and lamented at the temples, they decide to create a man as magnificent as Gilgamesh. The gods called this man Enkidu, and they allowed him to grow up in the wild amongst the animals. One day, a hunter comes across Enkidu. The hunter decides to send a prostitute from the temple to tame the wild man. In ancient times, it was believed that sexual relations could calm and domesticate a man, enticing him to become a civilized person.

Enkidu became a part of civilization and was taught by the prostitute how to be a rational human being. One day, Enkidu hears gossip about King Gilgamesh's cruelty and travels to Uruk to challenge the king to become a better ruler. When he arrives in Uruk, he sees Gilgamesh about to force himself into the bedchamber of a new bride. Enkidu places himself in front of the king, blocking the door. Gilgamesh attacks Enkidu, and the two men wrestle fiercely. In the end, Gilgamesh wins. The fight results in a brotherly friendship between the two men.

The new friends decide they need to strengthen their bond by sharing adventures, and they look around for something to challenge them. Their first adventure involves stealing trees from a forest forbidden to mortals. In the cedar forest, they encounter the evil and fearsome demon Humbaba. Humbaba is devoted to the god Enlil, the god of air, wind, and earth. The two strong men wrestle with the monster, and with the help of the sun god Shamash, they defeat Humbaba. As part of their exploits, the two chop down cedar trees and make a raft. With the wood of the biggest tree, they build a huge gate, which Enkidu plans to place at the entrance of Enlil's temple.

Eventually, King Gilgamesh and his friend Enkidu sail back to Uruk. The goddess Ishtar looked lustfully upon the magnificent Gilgamesh and tried to entice him into a relationship. Gilgamesh is not interested in the goddess, though. Enraged, Ishtar asks her father, Anu, the sky god, to command the "Bull of Heaven" to descend to Earth and kill Gilgamesh. The Bull of Heaven brings seven years of famine upon the Earth, so Gilgamesh and Enkidu have to fight him to save civilization. These two strong warriors kill the bull after a gruesome fight.

However, the council of gods is angered by this and decides the two should be taught a lesson. As punishment, they inflict Enkidu with a disease. Enkidu suffers from pain and hallucinations. He tells Gilgamesh about his visions of the netherworld. Gilgamesh is devasted when Enkidu dies, and he cannot stop himself from grieving for his friend.

Enkidu's visions of the netherworld plague Gilgamesh, who starts thinking about the possibility of his own demise. He decides to discard his royal garments and wear animal skins as a tribute to Enkidu. Gilgamesh travels through the wilderness to the edge of the world to find Utnapishtim, the Mesopotamian equivalent of Noah. He had been granted eternal life after the Great Flood. Gilgamesh is determined to learn how to cheat death and never end up in the netherworld.

Upon Gilgamesh's arrival at Mashu, a mountain with two peaks, two immortal scorpion monsters confront him. After begging them for passage, they finally relent. Gilgamesh enters the dark tunnel of torments, and when he emerges, he is faced with a magnificent view of a garden and a sea.

Gilgamesh goes down the mountain pass until he meets a tavern keeper. The veiled female, Siduri, listens to King Gilgamesh and his story. She explains to him that mortality is a blessing and that his quest for immortality will amount to nothing. However, she is not able to persuade him to give up his search.

Siduri shows Gilgamesh where to find the ferryman, Urshanabi, who will take him across the "Waters of Death" to find Utnapishtim. Eventually, Gilgamesh finds Utnapishtim, who tells him about the Great Flood sent by the gods to destroy all of humanity and how he was saved.

King Gilgamesh insists that he wants to become immortal, and Utnapishtim tests him by telling him that he needs to stay awake for an entire week. Gilgamesh fails miserably. Utnapishtim is disappointed in Gilgamesh and tells him that it is foolish to think he can stay awake for eternity if he cannot even stay awake for one week.

In the end, Utnapishtim convinces Gilgamesh to put on his royal robes and become a king his people can admire. Utnapishtim's wife understands the king's plight and asks her husband to show Gilgamesh the plant that brings eternal youth. Gilgamesh takes a piece of the plant and goes back home to Uruk. Along the way, he grows tired and falls asleep under a tree. A snake notices that Gilgamesh has fallen asleep. It slithers toward him and takes the plant. When Gilgamesh awakes, he realizes the plant is gone forever. Any chance of remaining young has gone as well.

Gilgamesh knows he has traveled to the ends of the Earth to return with nothing, yet he has reconciled himself with the fact of mortality. He realizes he cannot live forever, but now his eyes are opened to the magnificence of the city he has built and the enduring achievements of the people.

King Gilgamesh is ultimately revered for his building achievements and for bringing the lost knowledge of ancient times that he learned from Utnapishtim back to Uruk. There are many variations of the *Epic of Gilgamesh*, but regardless of the exact wording, he is seen as the first hero of all time.

The Creation Story – The *Eridu Genesis*

The creation myth was found in Nippur, a city in ancient Mesopotamia that was founded around 5000 BCE. Sumerian clay tablets tell the story of how people were created. Unfortunately, many parts of the original text are missing, and scholars had to use later versions to reconstruct the missing pieces.

According to the extant texts of the creation myth, human-like gods inhabited Earth in the beginning. When they ascended down to Earth, there was a lot of work that needed to be done. The gods worked hard and made the ground habitable by mining minerals and toiling in the soil to make the land arable to produce crops. After some time, the human-like gods became aggravated by the vast amount of work that had to be done, and they complained to the father of the gods, An.

An agreed and listened to the advice of his son Enki, who proposed that they create humans who could toil the earth instead of the gods. Together, Enki and his sister Ninki killed a lesser god and mixed his blood with clay from the fertile soil of Earth to create the first human.

These new beings were unable to reproduce, but Enki and Ninki modified the new being so he could function independently without the help of the gods. They called this man Adapa. This angered Enlil, Enki's brother, as he was not consulted. A conflict between the brothers started.

Enlil became man's biggest adversary. He put humankind through suffering and hardships. Since he was the god of the air, wind, and earth, he could create drought and floods.

In the *Epic of Gilgamesh*, the gods lived in a beautiful garden, similar to the biblical Garden of Eden, between the Tigris and Euphrates Rivers. The term "Eden" is actually Sumerian and means "flat terrain."

Other versions tell of a massive flood planned by the gods to destroy humankind because their noise was bothersome. To preserve life and start a new line of humanity, some gods decided that one man should be selected to save his family. He was also told to save every kind of animal and plant. The man was instructed to build a huge boat for himself, his family, the animals, and the plants to save them from drowning in the flood.

Utnapishtim

In one version of the *Epic of Gilgamesh*, the man who was saved from the flood was named Utnapishtim.

According to this account, the god Enlil cannot sleep because of the noise the humans were making in the city of Shurrupak on the Euphrates River. Enlil confers with the other gods, and they agree with him. The constant noise is too much, so they decide to flood the Earth and destroy mankind. The gods take an oath not to warn the humans and depart, satisfied with the outcome.

However, Ea visits Utnapishtim, a pious man, in a dream and tells him to build a boat. He gives Utnapishtim exact dimensions for the boat's size and instructs him to put his family and every animal on Earth to survive the coming flood.

Utnapishtim agrees but asks what he should tell the rest of the people when they inquire why he is building such a large boat. Ea tells him to say that the god Enlil is angry with him and that he may no longer live amongst the people.

The boat is built, and just in time. Adad, the god of storms, soon unleashes a terrifying storm of such proportions that even the other gods are afraid. The queen of heaven, Ishtar, cannot believe that she agreed to this terrible event. The storm rages for six days and six nights and then abates.

Utnapishtim first releases a dove, then a swallow, but both come back, having found no place to rest. Finally, he sends out a raven. It does not return.

Utnapishtim offers a sacrifice of cedar, cane, and myrtle, which he burns in a large cauldron on top of Mount Nisir. Ishtar calls the other gods to gather around the pleasing aroma. When Enlil arrives, he is angry that Utnapishtim and his family have survived. He asks how they knew to be prepared. Ea condemns Enlil for the grand punishment he had afflicted upon the world. The punishment did not fit the crime, and Enlil understands this after talking with the other gods. He goes to Utnapishtim, blessing him and his wife with immortality.

Enki and the World Order

The Sumerian god Enki's name translates to "En," meaning "lord," and "ki," meaning earth. It is commonly accepted that he was the "lord of the earth." He was also known by the name "E-A," meaning "lord of water." Enki was the patron deity of the city-state Eridu, and the origins of his name might be linked to Abzu, not Enki (with "Ab" meaning water).

Eridu was believed by the later Sumerians to be the first city in the world. It was the place where humans were created and where law and order were taught to humans. Later, Eridu became known as the city of the first kings. As such, it remained an important cult and religious center for thousands of years. Since Enki, the god of wisdom and intellect, was the patron god of this city, it was thought that Enki originally bestowed the *meh* (the practices and institutions that will make them civilized, such as, for example, kingship, sexual intercourse, and the arts) on the Sumerians.

Enki's temple at Eridu, known as E-Abzu, House of Abzu, or House of the Subterranean Waters, had a pool at the entrance. This majestic temple was the design that most Sumerian temples followed, which helps to confirm Eridu was the first city in Sumer.

The myth of Enki and the world order is complex and based on the Sumerian texts that were preserved on old Babylonian clay tablets. These texts describe events during the 3rd millennium BCE when Enki's temple in Eridu would have been the most important.

Enki's altruism and benevolence for humans and Earth are described in great detail in this myth. Enki is described as the "lord who walks nobly on heaven and earth and is beloved and self-reliant." His father, the sky god An, and his older brother, Enlil, praise Enki for his character and goodness. He is a most beloved son and brother.

In the myth, Eridu becomes the home of Enki and is described as the noblest house, the mast of heaven and Earth, and a place of beauty and peace. Enki derives his powers of fertility from the sweet underground waters of Abzu, and he teaches the people how to serve food at the tables of gods and humans. Enki is accompanied by seven sages who teach humanity about civilization, including mathematics and computing the numbers of the stars. Enlil greatly trusts Enki, and he is given praise and authority by Enlil to organize the world for the good of the rulers and humanity as a whole.

Enlil gathers all the *meh*, the measures of power in heaven and on Earth, and places them in the hands of Enki. Enki passes the *meh* to Eridu and then travels to all the Sumerian city-states to share the *meh* with them.

Enki establishes civilization and order on Earth. The idea behind all of this is for the deities, city-states, and neighbors of Sumer to work together as one to ensure peace and the continuation of humankind.

Conclusion

Allow your imagination to wander to the geographical area of Mesopotamia. Most of it lies in modern-day Iraq. Much of it is arid with little water, plenty of dried-up river beds, and lots of sand. It can become extremely hot in most areas. It is definitely not the perfect location for an emerging civilization to settle. So, how did this area become known as the Cradle of Civilization?

Today, it is evident from archaeological and other studies that in ancient times, some areas, especially between and around the Euphrates and Tigris Rivers, were much different. Possible seasonal settlements could have started as early as the 11th millennium BCE. Date palm remains date back to around 10,000 BCE. Oak trees, like those featured in the *Epic of Gilgamesh*, were present in antiquity and probably disappeared because of humans.

Archaeological excavations and ancient texts provide proof that the ancient people who created the world's first civilization were innovative, energetic, and brilliant. Is it perhaps due to the scarcity of some resources and the abundance of others that the people had to develop innovations? It is hard to imagine them prospering without overcoming hurdles as time passed and as the climate changed. In any event, the Sumerians thrived for millennia before they disappeared and were forgotten.

The year was 1842. Paul-Émile Botta, a naturalist, was the French consul general based in Mosul. He spent a year digging and searching mounds in Kuyunjik, only to discover some alabaster and mudbricks. Locals who worked alongside Botta on excavations told him about a mound in Khorsabad, which was a little more than twelve miles (twenty kilometers) away. He started excavating this mound, which turned out to be the ruins of the royal palace of Sargon II of the Neo Assyrian Empire. Botta found large reliefs and sculptures that referred to the town of Nineveh.

His head was in turmoil. What did he just unearth? Could this be evidence confirming the Bible? At this time, many treasure hunters and biblical scholars were searching for the lands of the biblical patriarch Abraham (Ibrahim).

The French government was jubilant over this discovery. It set in motion archaeological interest in the region, and France supplied Botta with resources and nine more archaeologists. Among them was Austen Henry Layard. Layard is best remembered for his unbelievable discovery of the Library of Ashurbanipal in ancient Nineveh, across the Tigris from Mosul in Iraq.

Sir Charles Leonard Woolley, an archaeologist who excavated the Hittite city of Carchemish between 1912 and 1914, was posted to Cairo during World War I. After the war, in the early 1920s, he and a team of archaeologists from the University of Pennsylvania and the British Museum went on a mission to uncover archaeological evidence of the ancient Sumerians.

They began to unravel the mysteries of this lost civilization in the cemeteries uncovered in and around Ur. The magnificent grave goods discovered at the cemetery, which Woolley named the Royal Cemetery of Ur, convinced archaeologists that they were dealing with a highly developed and civilized society of great importance.

Answers were found, but the answers only seemed to lead to more questions. No wonder so much of the discovered information about the Sumerian civilization is referred to as the "Sumerian

Problem" in scholarly circles. There is just no consensus, and too much is based on too little factual confirmation, such as the issue of applying pottery chronology across the ancient Near East to correlate dates.

In this book, we looked at where the Sumerians came from and where they settled. We saw how their settlements became the first cities of Eridu, Uruk, Ur, and Lagash.

We learned how they developed a calendar, hydraulic irrigation, agricultural implements, and the wheel. Where would we be today without the invention of the wheel?

We were even confronted with the first evidence of urban warfare: the battle between Hamoukar and Uruk. It is sad to think about how humanity has not progressed much in that regard and that pits are still being dug for mass burials. But warfare seems to be another aspect of being human, and it is yet another thing that connects us with this ancient civilization.

We saw how the first empire was created. Sargon was a great emperor who conquered lands and people as he saw fit. Yet, his daughter, Enheduanna, was the first known poet. She was- a priestess and an adoring child who honored her father with her words. And although not all families get along, the bond of a family unit was felt thousands of years ago.

One brother usurped the throne after his father's death and was assassinated after a short but brutal rule. When his sibling, Manishtushu, took the throne, we can see the same patterns of bribery and corruption that we experience today.

It is easy to think we are set apart from people who lived long ago. But that is far from the truth. Society today has built upon the amazing advancements of ancient people, and it is always worth exploring more of ancient history to better understand how humanity has progressed through the ages. Hopefully, this book has given you a taste of that. We encourage you to learn more about the people who came before us so you can better understand the world around you today.

Here's another book by Enthralling History that you might like

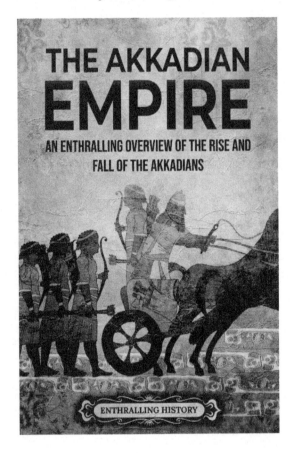

Free limited time bonus

Stop for a moment. We have a free bonus set up for you. The problem is this: we forget 90% of everything that we read after 7 days. Crazy fact, right? Here's the solution: we've created a printable, 1-page pdf summary for this book that you're reading now. All you have to do to get your free pdf summary is to go to the following website: **https://livetolearn.lpages.co/enthrallinghistory/**

Once you do, it will be intuitive. Enjoy, and thank you!

Bibliography

References used throughout

Books

Oxford Encyclopedia of Archaeology in the Near East, Oxford University Press, pp 476 – 483, E.M. Meyers (ed) 1997

Peoples of the Old Testament, Oxford University Press, 1973, D.J Wiseman (ed)

The History and Culture of Ancient Western Asia and Egypt, The Dorsey Press, U.S.A, A Bernard Knapp (ed)

Academic sites used throughout

"(PDF) Re-evaluating the Ubaid: Synchronizing the 6th and 5th millennia." https://www.academia.edu/3751066/Re_evaluating_the_Ubaid_Synchronizing_the_6th_and_5th_millennia_BC_of_Mesopotamia_and_the_Levant_unpublished_MA_thesis_.

"paper: Re-evaluating the Ubaid: Synchronizing the 6th and 5th millennia." 18 Aug. 2020, https://raisinguppharaoh.com/tag/paper-re-evaluating-the-ubaid-synchronizing-the-6th-and-5th-millennia-bc-of-mesopotamia-and-the-levant-77/.

"In search of the genetic footprints of Sumerians: a survey of Y." 04 Oct. 2011, https://www.ncbi.nlm.nih.gov/pmc/articles/PMC3215667/.

"NEW INSIGHTS ON THE ROLE OF ENVIRONMENTAL DYNAMICS SHAPING SOUTHERN." 18 Jul. 2019, https://www.cambridge.org/core/journals/iraq/article/new-insights-on-the-role-of-environmental-dynamics-shaping-southern-mesopotamia-from-the-preubaid-to-the-early-islamic-period/F7084E4BF1171D8B77021B286BFE300C.

"[PDF] NEW INSIGHTS ON THE ROLE OF ENVIRONMENTAL DYNAMICS SHAPING." 18 Jul. 2019, https://www.semanticscholar.org/paper/NEW-INSIGHTS-ON-THE-ROLE-OF-ENVIRONMENTAL-DYNAMICS-Altaweel-Marsh/67e4667f914d7f1b2b6966178f110a8cb629806d.

"AFTER THE UBAID: INTERPRETING CHANGE FROM THE CAUCASUS TO MESOPOTAMIA." https://www.academia.edu/5665737/AFTER_THE_UBAID_INTERPRETING_CHANGE_FROM_THE_CAUCASUS_TO_MESOPOTAMIA_AT_THE_DAWN_OF_URBAN_CIVILIZATION_4500_3500_BC_OFFPRINT.

"Carter 2016_Review of Marro After the Ubaid.pdf - academia.edu." https://www.academia.edu/35253069/Carter_2016_Review_of_Marro_After_the_Ubaid_pdf.

"Marro C. (ed.) 2012. After the Ubaid: Interpreting change." https://www.persee.fr/doc/paleo_0153-9345_2016_num_42_2_5729.

Web References

"Leonard Woolley (Author of The Sumerians) - Goodreads." https://www.goodreads.com/author/show/171163.Leonard_Woolley.

"Sir Leonard Woolley and the Excavations in Ur - SciHi Blog." 17 Apr. 2021, http://scihi.org/leonard-woolley-excavations-ur/.

"Woolley's Excavations - UrOnline." http://www.ur-online.org/about/woolleys-excavations/.

"Thorkild Jacobsen (Author of The Treasures of Darkness)." 02 May. 1993,

https://www.goodreads.com/author/show/166860.Thorkild_Jacobsen.

"Selected Writings of Samuel Noah Kramer - Internet Archive." 30 Mar. 2019, https://archive.org/details/KramerStudies19461990.

"THE SUMERIANS - Oriental Institute." https://oi.uchicago.edu/sites/oi.uchicago.edu/files/uploads/shared/docs/sumerians.pdf.

"Sumerian Mythology Index - Sacred-Texts.com." https://www.sacred-texts.com/ane/sum/.

"Samuel Noah Kramer | Open Library." 30 Sept. 2020, https://openlibrary.org/authors/OL398202A/Samuel_Noah_Kramer.

"The Sumerians: Their History, Culture, and Character." https://oi.uchicago.edu/research/publications/misc/sumerians-their-history-culture-and-character.

"AS 20. Sumerological Studies in Honor of Thorkild Jacobsen on His Seventieth Birthday." https://oi.uchicago.edu/research/publications/as/20-sumerological-studies-honor-thorkild-jacobsen-his-seventieth-birthday.

"THE SUMERIANS - The Oriental Institute of the University of Chicago." https://oi.uchicago.edu/sites/oi.uchicago.edu/files/uploads/shared/docs/sumerians.pdf.

"Nippur - The Oriental Institute of the University of Chicago." https://oi.uchicago.edu/research/projects/nippur-sacred-city-enlil-0.

"Cuneiform Studies | Near Eastern Languages and Civilizations."
https://nelc.uchicago.edu/cuneiform-studies.

"The Sumerians - University of Chicago Press."
https://press.uchicago.edu/ucp/books/book/chicago/S/bo27481022.html.

"Expedition Magazine - Penn Museum."
https://www.penn.museum/sites/expedition/ur-and-its-treasures/.

Chapter 1

"The Ubaid Period (5500–4000 B.C.) | Essay | The Metropolitan Museum of Art."
https://www.metmuseum.org/toah/hd/ubai/hd_ubai.htm.

"Ubaid Period | Mesopotamian history | Britannica."
https://www.britannica.com/topic/Ubaid-Period.

"Ubaidian Culture and the Roots of Mesopotamia - ThoughtCo." 07 Sept. 2018,
https://www.thoughtco.com/ubaidian-culture-ubaid-roots-mesopotamia-173089.

"Ubaid period - Wikipedia."
https://en.wikipedia.org/wiki/Ubaid_period.

"Cultures | Ubaid Period - Ancient Mesopotamia."
https://ancientmesopotamia.org/cultures/ubaid-period.php.

"Ancient Reptilians: The Unanswered Mystery of the 7,000-Year-Old Ubaid Lizardmen." 26 Feb. 2022, https://www.ancient-origins.net/unexplained-phenomena/ubaid-lizardmen-001116.

"Ubaid Period: Culture & Explanation | Study.com." 06 Feb. 2022,
https://study.com/academy/lesson/ubaid-period-culture-lesson-quiz.html.

"Tell al-Ubaid - Academic Dictionaries and Encyclopedias."
https://mesopotamia_enc.en-academic.com/360/Tell_al-Ubaid.

"Tall al-'Ubayd | archaeological site, Iraq | Britannica."
https://www.britannica.com/place/Tall-al-Ubayd.

"TELL AL-'UBAID."

https://rootshunt.com/angirasgautam/archaeologicalsitesiniraq/tellal
ubaid/tellalubaid.htm.

"Hereafter - Tell al-Ubaid - Our Ancient World."

http://ourancientworld.com/Settlement.aspx?id=81.

"Tel al 'Ubaid Ceramics: Photographs from Neutron Activation
Analysis."

https://core.tdar.org/image/373029/tel-al-ubaid-ceramics-
photographs.

"Tell al-'Ubaid Copper Lintel – Joy of Museums Virtual Tours."

https://joyofmuseums.com/museums/united-kingdom-
museums/london-museums/british-museum/tell-al-ubaid-copper-
lintel/.

"Tell al-'Ubaid Wiki." https://everipedia.org/Tell_al-%2560Ubaid.

"Tell al-'Ubaid | Detailed Pedia." 24 May. 2022,
https://www.detailedpedia.com/wiki-Tell_al-%27Ubaid.

Chapter 2

"Fertile Crescent - HISTORY." 20 Dec. 2017,
https://www.history.com/topics/pre-history/fertile-crescent.

"Fertile Crescent | National Geographic Society." 20 May. 2022,

https://www.nationalgeographic.org/encyclopedia/fertile-crescent/.

"Fertile Crescent | Definition, Location, Map, Significance, &
Facts."

https://www.britannica.com/place/Fertile-Crescent.

"The Sumerians of the Fertile Crescent."
https://www.gardencity.k12.ny.us/cms/lib/NY01913305/Centricity/D
omain/671/8%20Mesopotamia.pdf

"A Functional and Fertile Crescent: Technological Advancements."
03 Aug. 2018,

https://www.ancient-origins.net/history-important-events/fertile-crescent-0010488.

"Fertile Crescent - Cradle of Civilization (Collection) - World
History." 23 Nov. 2018,

https://www.worldhistory.org/collection/26/fertile-crescent---cradle-of-civilization/.

"The White Temple and the Great Ziggurat in the Mesopotamian
City of Uruk." 17 Oct. 2016, https://www.ancient-origins.net/ancient-places-asia/white-temple-and-great-ziggurat-mesopotamian-city-uruk-006835.

"Art: Ruins of the White Temple and Ziggurat - Annenberg
Learner."

https://www.learner.org/series/art-through-time-a-global-view/the-urban-experience/ruins-of-the-white-temple-and-ziggurat/.

"White Temple of God Anu in Sacred Precinct of Kullaba at Uruk."
10 Oct. 2016,

https://www.ancientpages.com/2016/10/10/white-temple-of-god-anu-in-sacred-precinct-of-kullaba-at-uruk/.

"Uruk - Wikipedia." https://en.wikipedia.org/wiki/Uruk.

"The White Temple - Artefacts." https://www.artefacts-berlin.de/portfolio-item/uruk-visualisation-project-the-white-temple/.

"Reconstruction of the White Temple – Ancient Art." 24 Apr. 2015,

https://ancientart.as.ua.edu/reconstruction-of-the-white-temple/.

"Hamoukar (Syria) | Jason Ur - Harvard University."

https://scholar.harvard.edu/jasonur/pages/hamoukar.

"Hamoukar, Great City of Old – StMU Research Scholars." 15 Sept.
2016,

https://stmuscholars.org/hamoukar-great-city-of-old/.

"Evidence of battle at Hamoukar points to early urban development."

http://chronicle.uchicago.edu/070118/hamoukar.shtml.

"Is it true the first known battle was in Hamoukar? If it is, why did it occur, and who were the combatants?" https://www.quora.com/Is-it-true-the-first-known-battle-was-in-Hamoukar-If-it-is-why-did-it-occur-and-who-were-the-combatants.

"Hamoukar - Wikipedia." https://en.wikipedia.org/wiki/Hamoukar.

"The Lost City of Hamoukar | Edward Willett." https://edwardwillett.com/2000/05/the-lost-city-of-hamoukar/.

"Site of Earliest Known Urban Warfare Threatened by Syrian War." 24 Jun. 2013,

https://www.livescience.com/37672-ancient-urban-warfare-site-threatened.html.

"Hamoukar - Oriental Institute."

https://oi.uchicago.edu/sites/oi.uchicago.edu/files/uploads/shared/docs/08-09_Hamoukar.pdf.

"Uruk - World History Encyclopedia." 28 Apr. 2011, https://www.worldhistory.org/uruk/.

"Uruk Period Mesopotamia: The Rise of Sumer - ThoughtCo." 21 Apr. 2019, https://www.thoughtco.com/uruk-period-mesopotamia-rise-of-sumer-171676.

"Cultures | Uruk Period - Ancient Mesopotamia." https://ancientmesopotamia.org/cultures/uruk-period.php.

"Uruk period - Wikipedia." https://en.wikipedia.org/wiki/Uruk_period.

"Tell Brak Home." https://www.tellbrak.mcdonald.cam.ac.uk/.

"Tell Brak (Syria) | Jason Ur - Harvard University." https://scholar.harvard.edu/jasonur/pages/tell-brak.

"Tell Brak - Wikipedia." https://en.wikipedia.org/wiki/Tell_Brak.

"Tell Brak - Mesopotamian Capital in Syria - ThoughtCo." 08 Mar. 2017,

https://www.thoughtco.com/tell-brak-mesopotamian-capital-syria-170274.

"Syria: Tell Brak - World Archaeology." 28 Apr. 2012,
https://www.world-archaeology.com/features/syria-tell-brak-3/.

Chapter 3

"Early Dynastic Period of Sumer - Ancient Mesopotamia."

https://ancientmesopotamia.org/cultures/early-dynastic-period-of-sumer.php.

"Sumer - HISTORY." 07 Dec. 2017,
https://www.history.com/topics/ancient-middle-east/sumer.

"Sumer Timeline - World History Encyclopedia."
https://www.worldhistory.org/timeline/sumer/.

"Ancient Sumer & The Sumerian Civilization: Here's What We
Know." 02 Dec. 2020, https://www.thecollector.com/ancient-sumer-civilization/.

"EARLY DYNASTIC/AKKADIAN/UR III SUMER: 2."
https://www.unm.edu/~gbawden/328-rel/328-rel.htm.

"Early Dynastic Sumer Research Papers - Academia.edu."

https://www.academia.edu/Documents/in/Early_Dynastic_Sumer?page=5.

"Sumer (Early Dynastic Period) with Assyrian Border Style 11." 27
Sept. 2021,
https://archive.org/details/SumerEarlyDynasticPeriodArabicWithAssyrianBorderStyle11.

"Early Dynastic Sumer Research Papers - Academia.edu."

https://www.academia.edu/Documents/in/Early_Dynastic_Sumer?page=3.

"Cultures | Early Dynastic Period of Sumer."
https://ancientmesopotamia.org/cultures/early-dynastic-period-of-sumer.

"Early Dynastic Period (Mesopotamia) - Wikipedia."
https://en.wikipedia.org/wiki/Early_Dynastic_Period_(Mesopotamia).

"Old Sumerian Period (c. 3000 BC - Ancient Civilizations."
https://anciv.info/mesopotamia/old-sumerian-period.html.

"Sumer (Early Dynastic Period) with Assyrian Border Style 11." 27 Sept. 2021,

https://archive.org/details/SumerEarlyDynasticPeriodArabicWithAssyrianBorderStyle11.

"Sumerian Religion - The Spiritual Life." https://slife.org/sumerian-religion/.

"Jemdet Nasr - Oxford Reference."
https://www.oxfordreference.com/view/10.1093/oi/authority.20110803100019282.

"List of Place Names from Jemdet Nasr (Illustration) - World History." 07 Apr. 2016,
https://www.worldhistory.org/image/4852/list-of-place-names-from-jemdet-nasr/.

"Historic Overview of Early Mesopotamian Civilization."
https://www.unm.edu/~gbawden/328-sumhist/328-sumhist.htm.

"Defining the style of the period: Jemedt Nasr, 1926-28."

https://ehrafarchaeology.yale.edu/ehrafa/citation.do?method=citation&forward=browseAuthorsFullContext&id=mh62-001.

"Jemdet Nasr: a Pleiades place resource."
https://pleiades.stoa.org/places/733910291.

"The Jemdet-Nasr Period - Penn Museum."

https://www.penn.museum/documents/publications/bulletin/10-3_4/jemdet-nasr_period.pdf.

"Jemdet Nasr: The Site and the Period | The Biblical Archaeologist
https://www.journals.uchicago.edu/doi/10.2307/3210314.

"Jemdet Nasr Period - 3300-2900 BC - GlobalSecurity.org." 07 Sept. 2011,

https://www.globalsecurity.org/military/world/iraq/history-jemdet-nasr.htm.

"Jemdet Nasr - Wikipedia."
https://en.wikipedia.org/wiki/Jemdet_Nasr.

"Mesannepada | ruler of Ur | Britannica."
https://www.britannica.com/biography/Mesannepada.

"Ancient Mesopotamian Gods and Goddesses - Mesopotamian history: the basics."
http://oracc.museum.upenn.edu/amgg/mesopotamianhistory/index.html.

"Sumerian King of the First Dynasty of Ur - Ancient Pages." 14 Apr. 2016,

https://www.ancientpages.com/2016/04/14/helmet-of-meskalamdug-sumerian-king-of-the-first-dynasty-of-ur/.

"List of Rulers of Mesopotamia | Lists of Rulers | Heilbrunn Timeline."

https://www.metmuseum.org/toah/hd/meru/hd_meru.htm.

"Ancient Mesopotamian Gods and Goddesses - An/Anu (god)."

http://oracc.museum.upenn.edu/amgg/listofdeities/an/index.html.

"History of Mesopotamia - First historical personalities | Britannica."

https://www.britannica.com/place/Mesopotamia-historical-region-Asia/First-historical-personalities.

"Mesannepada - Wikipedia."
https://en.wikipedia.org/wiki/Mesannepada.

"Ur-Nanshe | king of Lagash | Britannica."
https://www.britannica.com/biography/Ur-Nanshe.

"Sumerian People | Ur-Nanshe - Ancient Mesopotamia."
https://ancientmesopotamia.org/people/ur-nanshe.php.

"Ur-Nanshe - Wikipedia." https://en.wikipedia.org/wiki/Ur-Nanshe.

"Ur-Nanshe [CDLI Wiki]."
https://cdli.ox.ac.uk/wiki/doku.php?id=ur-nanshe.

"Sumerian Plaque Dedicated To King Ur-Nanshe, The Founder Of
The 1st Dynasty of Lagash." 05 Dec. 2018,
https://www.ancientpages.com/2018/12/05/sumerian-plaque-
dedicated-to-king-ur-nanshe-the-founder-of-the-1st-dynasty-of-
lagash/.

"Ur-Nanshe Biography - King of Lagash | Pantheon."
https://pantheon.world/profile/person/Ur-Nanshe/.

"Lagash | ancient city, Iraq | Britannica."
https://www.britannica.com/place/Lagash.

"Records of the Past, 2nd series, Vol. I: The Inscriptions of Telloh."
https://sacred-texts.com/ane/rp/rp201/rp20112.htm.

"Enmebaragesi | king of Kish | Britannica."
https://www.britannica.com/biography/Enmebaragesi.

"Enmebaragesi - Wikipedia."
https://en.wikipedia.org/wiki/Enmebaragesi.

"Enmebaragesi Biography - Ancient Mesopotamian king |
Pantheon."

https://pantheon.world/profile/person/Enmebaragesi/.

"Enmebaragesi, King of Kish - geni family tree." 06 Sept. 2016,

https://www.geni.com/people/Enmebaragesi-King-of-
Kish/6000000006277541149.

"8 kings descended from heaven and ruled for 241,200 years." 08 May. 2022,

https://mysteriesrunsolved.com/2020/11/the-sumerian-king-list-8-kings-ruled-241200-years.html.

"History of Mesopotamia - First historical personalities | Britannica."

https://www.britannica.com/place/Mesopotamia-historical-region-Asia/First-historical-personalities.

"Holy City of God Enlil and One of the Oldest Cities of Sumer, Ancient Pages." 08 Jun. 2020,

https://www.ancientpages.com/2020/06/08/nippur-holy-city-of-god-enlil-and-one-of-the-oldest-cities-of-sumer/.

"Kish | ancient city, Iraq | Britannica."
https://www.britannica.com/place/Kish.

Chapter 4

"The Akkadian Period (ca. 2350–2150 B.C.) | Essay | The Metropolitan Museum of Art."

https://www.metmuseum.org/toah/hd/akka/hd_akka.htm.

"Mesopotamian art and architecture - Akkadian period | Britannica."

https://www.britannica.com/art/Mesopotamian-art/Akkadian-period.

"Akkadian Period - Oxford Reference."

https://www.oxfordreference.com/view/10.1093/oi/authority.20110803095359204.

"Cultures | Akkadian Empire - Ancient Mesopotamia."

https://ancientmesopotamia.org/cultures/akkadian-empire.php.

"Akkadian Empire - Wikipedia."
https://en.wikipedia.org/wiki/Akkadian_Empire.

"Explaining the Fall of the Great Akkadian Empire - Ancient Origins." 10 Jan. 2021, https://www.ancient-origins.net/ancient-places-asia/akkadian-empire-0011871.

"Chapter Six - Sealing Practices in the Akkadian Period."
https://www.cambridge.org/core/books/seals-and-sealing-in-the-ancient-world/sealing-practices-in-the-akkadian-period/81775349C1B2C3BD7E6567C21D9F9B74.

"The Akkadian Period: Empire, Environment, and Imagination."
https://www.lettere.uniroma1.it/sites/default/files/3109/6_MCMAHON%202012.pdf.

"(PDF) The Use of Sumerian and Akkadian during the Akkadian Period." 10 May. 2022,
https://www.academia.edu/78905915/The_Use_of_Sumerian_and_Akkadian_during_the_Akkadian_Period_The_Case_of_the_Elites_
.

"Akkad Timeline - World History Encyclopedia."
https://www.worldhistory.org/timeline/akkad/.

"Akkadian Empire: The first Semitic-speaking empire of Mesopotamia." 21 Mar. 2020, https://www.ancient-civilizations.com/akkadian-empire/.

"Cuneiform - Wikipedia." https://en.wikipedia.org/wiki/Cuneiform.

"Akkad | People, Culture, History, & Facts | Britannica."
https://www.britannica.com/place/Akkad.

"Akkad - World History Encyclopedia." 28 Apr. 2011,
https://www.worldhistory.org/akkad/.

"Akkad (city) - Wikipedia."
https://en.wikipedia.org/wiki/Akkad_(city).

"Akkadian Empire: The first Semitic-speaking empire of Mesopotamia." 21 Mar. 2020, https://www.ancient-civilizations.com/akkadian-empire/.

"The Akkadian Period (ca. 2350–2150 B.C.) | Essay | The Metropolitan Museum of Art." https://www.metmuseum.org/toah/hd/akka/hd_akka.htm.

"The history of AKKAD." http://akkad.org/.

"The Akkadian Empire - History." https://www.historyonthenet.com/the-akkadian-empire.

"Agade | ancient city, Iraq | Britannica." https://www.britannica.com/place/Agade.

"Kingdoms of Mesopotamia - Agade / Akkad - The History Files." https://www.historyfiles.co.uk/KingListsMiddEast/MesopotamiaAkkad.htm.

"About: Ur-Zababa." https://live.dbpedia.org/resource/Ur-Zababa.

"Sargon and Ur-Zababa | Mesopotamian Gods & Kings." http://www.mesopotamiangods.com/sargon-and-ur-zababa/.

"Ur-Zababa Biography | Pantheon." https://pantheon.world/profile/person/Ur-Zababa/.

"Ur-Zababa - Wikipedia." https://en.wikipedia.org/wiki/Ur-Zababa.

"Lugalzagesi | ruler of Uruk | Britannica." https://www.britannica.com/biography/Lugalzagesi.

"Lugal-zage-si - Wikipedia." https://en.wikipedia.org/wiki/Lugal-zage-si.

"Ambitious King Who United Sumer - Ancient Pages." 30 Apr. 2020, https://www.ancientpages.com/2020/04/30/infamous-end-of-lugalzagesi-ambitious-king-who-united-sumer/.

"King Sargon of Akkad—facts and information - Culture." 18 Jun. 2019, https://www.nationalgeographic.com/culture/article/king-sargon-akkad.

"Sargon of Akkad - Wikipedia." https://en.wikipedia.org/wiki/Sargon_of_Akkad.

"Sargon | History, Accomplishments, Facts, & Definition | Britannica." https://www.britannica.com/biography/Sargon.

"Sargon of Akkad: The Orphan Who Founded an Empire." 04 Mar. 2022, https://www.thecollector.com/sargon-of-akkad-akkadian-empire/.

"The Legend of Sargon of Akkad - World History Encyclopedia." 30 Aug. 2014, https://www.worldhistory.org/article/746/the-legend-of-sargon-of-akkad/.

"Sargon - Encyclopedia of The Bible - Bible Gateway." https://www.biblegateway.com/resources/encyclopedia-of-the-bible/Sargon.

"Sargon the Great and the World's First Professional Army." 18 Apr. 2016, https://warfarehistorynetwork.com/2016/04/18/professional-soldiers-king-sargon-of-akkads-expanding-empire/.

"Sargon of Agade - penn.museum." https://www.penn.museum/documents/publications/bulletin/10-3_4/sargon_agade.pdf.

"Enheduanna - New World Encyclopedia." https://www.newworldencyclopedia.org/entry/Enheduanna.

"Enheduanna - Poet, Priestess, Empire Builder - World History Encyclopedia." 12 Oct. 2010, https://www.worldhistory.org/article/190/enheduanna---poet-priestess-empire-builder/.

"Enheduanna – the world's first known author - World History Edu." 20 Mar. 2022, https://www.worldhistoryedu.com/enheduanna-the-worlds-first-known-author/.

"Enheduanna - Virginia Tech." https://cddc.vt.edu/feminism/Enheduanna.html.

"Enheduanna -The Akkadian Princess who became the world's first female author." 14 Feb. 2022, https://www.historyofroyalwomen.com/the-royal-women/enheduanna-the-akkadian-princess-who-became-the-worlds-first-female-author/.

"Elamite | Rimush." https://ancientmesopotamia.org/people/rimush.

"Rimush - Wikipedia." https://en.wikipedia.org/wiki/Rimush.

"Elamite | Rimush - Ancient Mesopotamia." https://ancientmesopotamia.org/people/rimush.php.

"Rimush, 2nd King of Akkadian Empire - Geni.com." 05 Apr. 2021, https://www.geni.com/people/Rimush-King-of-the-Akkadian-Empire/6000000047190539827.

"Rimush Biography | Pantheon." https://pantheon.world/profile/person/Rimush/.

"People | Manishtusu - Ancient Mesopotamia." https://ancientmesopotamia.org/people/manishtusu.php.

"Manishtushu - Wikipedia." https://en.wikipedia.org/wiki/Manishtushu.

"People | Manishtusu." https://ancientmesopotamia.org/people/manishtusu.

"Manishtusu | king of Akkad | Britannica." https://www.britannica.com/biography/Manishtusu.

"First Sumerian Revolt - Ancient Pages." 09 Nov. 2020, https://www.ancientpages.com/2020/11/09/story-behind-the-first-sumerian-revolt/.

"Manishtushu Biography | Pantheon." https://pantheon.world/profile/person/Manishtushu/.

"Naram-Sin - World History Encyclopedia." 07 Aug. 2014, https://www.worldhistory.org/Naram-Sin/.

"Naram-Sin of Akkad - Wikipedia." https://en.wikipedia.org/wiki/Naram-Sin_of_Akkad.

"Akkadian Empire - History - Origins - Naram-Sin | Technology Trends." https://www.primidi.com/akkadian_empire/history/origins/naram-sin.

"Naram Sin: Victory Stele & Concept | Study.com." 07 Feb. 2022, https://study.com/academy/lesson/naram-sin-victory-stele-lesson-quiz.html.

"Sumerian People | Naram-Sin - Ancient Mesopotamia." https://ancientmesopotamia.org/people/naram-sin.php.

"Shar-kali-sharri | king of Akkad | Britannica." https://www.britannica.com/biography/Shar-kali-sharri.

"Sumerian People | Shar-Kali-Sharri." https://ancientmesopotamia.org/people/shar-kali-sharri.

"Shar-Kali-Sharri - Wikipedia." https://en.wikipedia.org/wiki/Shar-Kali-Sharri.

"(DOC) Sargon and Shar-Kali-Sharri | Damien Mackey - Academia.edu." 08 Jun. 2019, https://www.academia.edu/39473281/Sargon_and_Shar_Kali_Sharri.

"MS 4556 - The Schoyen Collection." https://www.schoyencollection.com/history-collection-introduction/sumerian-history-collection/king-shar-kali-sharri-ms-4556.

"Shar-Kali-Sharri in Italian - English-Italian Dictionary | Glosbe." https://glosbe.com/en/it/Shar-Kali-Sharri.

Chapter 5

"Gutians - World History Encyclopedia." 27 Oct. 2021, https://www.worldhistory.org/Gutians/.

"Gutians." http://www.realhistoryww.com/world_history/ancient/Misc/Sumer/Gutians.htm.

"GUTIANS – Encyclopedia Iranica." 15 Dec. 2002, https://www.iranicaonline.org/articles/gutians.

"Cultures | Gutium - Ancient Mesopotamia." https://ancientmesopotamia.org/cultures/gutium.php.

"Gutian rule in Mesopotamia - Wikipedia." https://en.wikipedia.org/wiki/Gutian_rule_in_Mesopotamia.

"Kingdoms of Mesopotamia - Gutians / Gutium - The History Files." https://www.historyfiles.co.uk/KingListsMiddEast/MesopotamiaGutium.htm.

"Gutian people in Zagros mountains; pale in complexion and blonde." https://cof.quantumfuturegroup.org/events/5390.

"Gudea - The Gutians." http://realhistoryww.com/world_history/ancient/Sumer_Iraq_3.htm.

"Guti | people | Britannica." https://www.britannica.com/topic/Guti.

Chapter 6

"Ur-Nammu - World History Encyclopedia." 16 Jun. 2014, https://www.worldhistory.org/Ur-Nammu/.

"Ur-Nammu - Wikipedia." https://en.wikipedia.org/wiki/Ur-Nammu.

"The Code of Ur-Nammu: The Oldest Law in the World?." 04 May. 2022, https://www.historicmysteries.com/code-of-ur-nammu/.

"Ur-Nammu | king of Ur | Britannica." https://www.britannica.com/biography/Ur-Nammu.

"Code of Ur-Nammu - World History Encyclopedia." 26 Oct. 2021, https://www.worldhistory.org/Code_of_Ur-Nammu/.

"The Legacy of Ur-Nammu – History of Kurdistan." 09 Oct. 2016, http://historyofkurd.com/english/2016/10/09/the-legacy-of-ur-nammu/.

"Sumerian People | Ur-Nammu - Ancient Mesopotamia."

https://ancientmesopotamia.org/people/ur-nammu.php.

"The Code of Ur-Nammu: When Ancient Sumerians Laid Down the Law." 15 Sept. 2021, https://www.ancient-origins.net/artifacts-ancient-writings/code-ur-nammu-sumerians-009333.

"Utu-khegal | king of Uruk | Britannica." https://www.britannica.com/biography/Utu-khegal.

"Utu-hengal - Wikipedia." https://en.wikipedia.org/wiki/Utu-hengal.

"The Victory of Utu-hegal (Poem of Utu-ḫeĝal)." https://www.mesopotamiangods.com/poem-of-utu-%E1%B8%ABegal/.

"Vase of Utu-Hegal of Uruk - World History Encyclopedia." 28 Feb. 2018, https://www.worldhistory.org/image/8195/vase-of-utu-hegal-of-uruk/.

"Shulgi of Ur - World History Encyclopedia." 17 Jun. 2014, https://www.worldhistory.org/Shulgi_of_Ur/.

"Shulgi | king of Ur | Britannica." https://www.britannica.com/biography/Shulgi.

"Shulgi of Ur Timeline - World History Encyclopedia." https://www.worldhistory.org/timeline/Shulgi_of_Ur/.

"People | Shulgi." https://ancientmesopotamia.org/people/shulgi.

"The Mighty Deeds of King Shulgi of Ur, Master of Mesopotamian Monarchs." 11 Mar. 2019, https://www.ancient-origins.net/history-famous-people/king-shulgi-0011602.

"Shulgi - Forgotten Realms Wiki." https://forgottenrealms.fandom.com/wiki/Shulgi.

"Shulgi: First Great Athlete? | Ancient Greek Sport." 27 Feb. 2017, https://sites.psu.edu/camskines442/2017/02/27/shulgi-first-great-athlete/.

"Shulgi Biography - Sumerian King | Pantheon." https://pantheon.world/profile/person/Shulgi/.

"Shulgi - Wikipedia." https://en.wikipedia.org/wiki/Shulgi.

"Amar-Sin - Wikipedia." https://en.wikipedia.org/wiki/Amar-Sin.

"Shu-Sin | king of Ur | Britannica."
https://www.britannica.com/biography/Shu-Sin.

"The oldest love poem of the world | Arts & History." 30 Aug. 2015,

https://artsnhistory.com/2015/08/30/sumerian/.

"Shu-Sin - Wikipedia." https://en.wikipedia.org/wiki/Shu-Sin.

"A Door Socket with King Shu-Sin Inscription (Illustration) - World History." 25 Sept. 2014,

https://www.worldhistory.org/image/3083/a-door-socket-with-king-shu-sin-inscription/.

"DUMUZI - the Sumerian God of Farming (Mesopotamian mythology)."

https://www.godchecker.com/mesopotamian-mythology/DUMUZI/.

"Dumuzi-Abzu | Sumerian deity | Britannica."
https://www.britannica.com/topic/Dumuzi-Abzu.

"Dumuzi."
http://www.mesopotamia.co.uk/gods/explore/dumuzi.html.

"Dumuzi / Tammuz the Shepherd, Son to Enlil & Ninsun, Slide-Show."

https://www.mesopotamiangods.com/dumuzi-the-shepherd-son-to-enki-ninsun/.

Chapter 7

"Amorite | people | Britannica."
https://www.britannica.com/topic/Amorite.

"Cultures | Amorites - Ancient Mesopotamia."

https://ancientmesopotamia.org/cultures/amorites.php.

"What do we know about the Amorites? - CompellingTruth.org."

https://www.compellingtruth.org/Amorites.html.

"Amorites - Wikipedia." https://en.wikipedia.org/wiki/Amorites.

"Amorite - World History Encyclopedia." 28 Apr. 2011,
https://www.worldhistory.org/amorite/.

"Amorites, an introduction – Smarthistory." 06 Apr. 2022,
https://smarthistory.org/amorites-an-introduction/.

"Ebla | ancient city, Syria | Britannica."
https://www.britannica.com/place/Ebla.

"Ebla - Wikipedia." https://en.wikipedia.org/wiki/Ebla.

"Ebla - New World Encyclopedia."
https://www.newworldencyclopedia.org/entry/Ebla.

"Ebla in the Third Millennium B.C. | Essay | The Metropolitan
Museum of Art."
https://www.metmuseum.org/toah/hd/ebla/hd_ebla.htm.

"First Kingdoms: The Forgotten Mesopotamian Kingdom of Ebla."
21 May. 2019,

https://www.ancient-origins.net/ancient-places-asia/ebla-0011940.

"Ebla: Its Impact on Bible Records - Institute for Creation
Research."

https://www.icr.org/article/ebla-its-impact-bible-records/.

"Cultures | Ebla."
https://ancientmesopotamia.org/cultures/ebla.php.

"Shulgi | king of Ur | Britannica."
https://www.britannica.com/biography/Shulgi.

"Shulgi of Ur Timeline - World History Encyclopedia."
https://www.worldhistory.org/timeline/Shulgi_of_Ur/.

"The Mighty Deeds of King Shulgi of Ur, Master of Mesopotamian
Monarchs." 11 Mar. 2019,

https://www.ancient-origins.net/history-famous-people/king-shulgi-
0011602.

"SHULGI - mesopotamia.en-academic.com."
https://mesopotamia.en-academic.com/314/SHULGI.

"Shulgi - Wikipedia." https://en.wikipedia.org/wiki/Shulgi.

"Ibbi-Sin | king of Ur | Britannica."
https://www.britannica.com/biography/Ibbi-Sin.

"Ibbi-Sin - Wikipedia." https://en.wikipedia.org/wiki/Ibbi-Sin.

"Ibbi-Sin Biography | Pantheon."
https://pantheon.world/profile/person/Ibbi-Sin/.

"IBBI-SIN." https://mesopotamia.en-academic.com/182/IBBI-SIN.

"Martu - Wikipedia." https://en.wikipedia.org/wiki/Martu.

"Amurru (god) - Wikipedia."
https://en.wikipedia.org/wiki/Amurru_(god).

"Amurru | ancient district, Egypt | Britannica."
https://www.britannica.com/place/Amurru.

"Amarru: the home of the Northern Semites." 31 Dec. 2014,
https://archive.org/details/amarruhomeofnort00clay.

"Ur - Wikipedia." https://en.wikipedia.org/wiki/Ur.

"Ur - World History Encyclopedia." 28 Apr. 2011,
https://www.worldhistory.org/ur/.

"Ur | City, History, Ziggurat, Sumer, Mesopotamia, & Facts."
https://www.britannica.com/place/Ur.

"The Ancient City of Ur - HeritageDaily - Archaeology News." 05
Oct. 2020,
https://www.heritagedaily.com/2020/10/the-ancient-city-of-
ur/135753.

"Ur | Ur Region Archaeology Project."
https://www.urarchaeology.org/ur/.

"Ancient World History: City of Ur."
https://earlyworldhistory.blogspot.com/2012/01/city-of-ur.html.

"Ur, Sumeria. - Ancient-Wisdom." http://www.ancient-wisdom.com/iraqur.htm.

"Qatna, Syria - World Archaeology." 07 Jan. 2006, https://www.world-archaeology.com/features/qatna-syria/.

"The Kingdom of Qatna - HeritageDaily - Archaeology News." 29 May. 2020, https://www.heritagedaily.com/2020/05/the-kingdom-of-qatna/129581.

"Elam - World History Encyclopedia." 27 Aug. 2020, https://www.worldhistory.org/elam/.

"Elam | History, Definition, & Meaning | Britannica." https://www.britannica.com/place/Elam.

"Elam - Wikipedia." https://en.wikipedia.org/wiki/Elam.

"The Elamites - The Early History of Elam and Its People (Part 1)." 26 Aug. 2020, https://www.worldhistory.org/video/2088/the-elamites---the-early-history-of-elam-and-its/.

"Ancient World History: Medes, Persians, and Elamites." https://earlyworldhistory.blogspot.com/2012/03/medes-persians-and-elamites.html.

"Elamite Empire: Art & Culture | Study.com." https://study.com/academy/lesson/elamite-empire-art-culture.html.

"Publications - Matt Konfirst - Google Search." https://sites.google.com/site/mattkonfirst/publications.

"Did Climate Change Bring Sumerian Civilization to an End?." 05 Dec. 2012, https://www.biblicalarchaeology.org/daily/biblical-sites-places/biblical-archaeology-places/did-climate-change-bring-sumerian-civilization-to-an-end/.

"Acid rock drainage and climate change - ScienceDirect." 01 Feb. 2009,

https://www.sciencedirect.com/science/article/pii/S037567420800008
61.

"Climate Shift May Have Silenced Ancient Civilization - HuffPost."
04 Dec. 2012,

https://www.huffpost.com/entry/sumerian-language-drought-climate-change_n_2238058.

"Kindattu - Wikipedia." https://en.wikipedia.org/wiki/Kindattu.

"History of Mesopotamia - Ur III in decline

Britannica."https://www.britannica.com/place/Mesopotamia-historical-region-Asia/Ur-III-in-decline.

"People | Ibbi-Sin - Ancient Mesopotamia."
https://ancientmesopotamia.org/people/ibbi-sin.php.

Chapter 8

"Sumerian Language – Mesopotamia."
https://guides.lib.uw.edu/c.php?g=341420&p=2298733.

"The Sumerian King List and the Early History of Mesopotamia."

https://www.academia.edu/10052536/The_Sumerian_King_List_and_the_Early_History_of_Mesopotamia.

"Sumerian - Oxford Reference. The Sumerian King List - Livius."

https://www.livius.org/sources/content/anet/266-the-sumerian-king-list/.

"The Sumerian King List." https://rebirthoftheword.com/the-sumerian-king-list/.

"The Sumerian King list - Earth-history." 14 May. 2022,
https://earth-history.com/sumer/the-sumerian-king-list.

https://www.oxfordreference.com/view/10.1093/oi/authority.201108
03100541919.

"Sumerian King List - Wikipedia."
https://en.wikipedia.org/wiki/Sumerian_King_List.

"The Antediluvian Patriarchs and the Sumerian King List." 01 Dec. 1998,

https://answersingenesis.org/bible-history/the-antediluvian-patriarchs-and-the-sumerian-king-list/.

"15 facts about the Sumerian King List: When gods ruled Earth." 22 May. 2022,

https://www.ancient-code.com/15-facts-about-the-sumerian-king-list-when-gods-ruled-earth/.

"Was Alulim, First King of Sumer and Eridu Biblical Adam?." 14 Mar. 2019, https://www.ancientpages.com/2019/03/14/was-alulim-first-king-of-sumer-and-eridu-biblical-adam/.

"Alulim - Wikipedia." https://ro.wikipedia.org/wiki/Alulim.

"Hebrew Codec." https://yhvh.org/.

"Who Was the First King in the World? - WorldAtlas." 11 Mar. 2020,

https://www.worldatlas.com/who-was-the-first-king-in-the-world.html.

"Before the Great Deluge, Eighth Antediluvian Kings Ruled for 241,200 Years - Ancient Code." 20 Apr. 2022, https://www.ancient-code.com/before-the-great-deluge-eighth-antediluvian-kings-ruled-for-241200-years/.

"Mesopotamia - THE WORLD ALOHA." https://www.theworldaloha.com/world/mesopotamia.

"The Early Dynastic Period in Ancient Mesopotamia." 14 Oct. 2019, https://brewminate.com/the-early-dynastic-period-in-ancient-mesopotamia/.

"Mesh-ki-ang-gasher Biography - Sumerian ruler priest of Inanna."

https://pantheon.world/profile/person/Mesh-ki-ang-gasher.

"Meshkiangasher - Wikipedia."
https://en.wikipedia.org/wiki/Meshkiangasher.

"Enmerkar | Mesopotamian hero | Britannica."
https://www.britannica.com/biography/Enmerkar.

"Enmerkar - Wikipedia." https://en.wikipedia.org/wiki/Enmerkar.

"Enmerkar: Legendary Sumerian Founder and Ruler of Uruk and
Grandson of God Utu." 23 Mar. 2020,
https://www.ancientpages.com/2020/03/23/enmerkar-legendary-
sumerian-founder-and-ruler-of-uruk-and-grandson-of-god-utu/.

"Enmerkar and the Lord of Aratta | Mesopotamian Gods & Kings."

http://www.mesopotamiangods.com/enmerkar-and-the-lord-of-
aratta/.

"Enmerkar and the Lord of Aratta - TheAlmightyGuru." 28 Apr.
2020,

http://www.thealmightyguru.com/Wiki/index.php?title=Enmerkar_a
nd_the_Lord_of_Aratta.

"Enmerkar - Bible History." https://bible-
history.com/links/enmerkar-2556.

"Gilgamesh | Epic, Summary, & Facts | Britannica."
https://www.britannica.com/topic/Gilgamesh.

"Gilgamesh - World History Encyclopedia." 29 Mar. 2018,
https://www.worldhistory.org/gilgamesh/.

"Gilgamesh - Wikipedia." https://en.wikipedia.org/wiki/Gilgamesh.

"The Myth of Gilgamesh, Hero King of Mesopotamia -
ThoughtCo." 20 Aug. 2019,

https://www.thoughtco.com/gilgamesh-4766597.

"Epic of Gilgamesh - Ancient Texts."

http://www.ancienttexts.org/library/mesopotamian/gilgamesh/.

"The Epic of Gilgamesh | World Epics - Columbia University."

https://edblogs.columbia.edu/worldepics/project/gilgamesh/.

"What the Bible says about Gilgamesh."

https://www.bibletools.org/index.cfm/fuseaction/Topical.show/RTD/CGG/ID/775/Gilgamesh.htm.

"BBC NEWS | Science/Nature | Gilgamesh tomb believed found." 29 Apr. 2003,

http://news.bbc.co.uk/2/hi/science/nature/2982891.stm.

"Gilgamesh | Essay | The Metropolitan Museum of Art | Heilbrunn Timeline." https://www.metmuseum.org/toah/hd/gilg/hd_gilg.htm.

"Queen Kubaba: The Tavern Keeper Who Became the First Female Ruler in History." 23 Feb. 2021, https://www.discovermagazine.com/planet-earth/queen-kubaba-the-tavern-keeper-who-became-the-first-female-ruler-in-history.

"Brooklyn Museum: Kubaba."

https://www.brooklynmuseum.org/eascfa/dinner_party/heritage_floor/kubaba.

"All Hail the Divine Ruler, Queen of Kish - ThoughtCo." 30 May. 2019,

https://www.thoughtco.com/kubaba-a-queen-among-kings-121164.

"Kubaba | Anatolian deity | Britannica." https://www.britannica.com/topic/Kubaba.

"Queen Kubaba: The Tavern Keeper Who Became the First Female Ruler in History." 08 Mar. 2022, https://headtopics.com/us/queen-kubaba-the-tavern-keeper-who-became-the-first-female-ruler-in-history-24609982.

"Ku-Bau: The First Woman Ruler – Semiramis-Speaks.com." 10 Dec. 2011, http://semiramis-speaks.com/ku-bau-the-first-woman-ruler/.

"Kubaba — Google Arts & Culture." https://artsandculture.google.com/entity/m04dk_d.

"Kubaba (goddess) - Wikipedia." https://en.wikipedia.org/wiki/Kubaba_(goddess).

"Kubaba - Wikipedia." https://en.wikipedia.org/wiki/Kubaba.

"Eannatum | king of Lagash | Britannica."
https://www.britannica.com/biography/Eannatum.

"People | Eannatum."
https://ancientmesopotamia.org/people/eannatum.

"Eannatum - Wikipedia." https://en.wikipedia.org/wiki/Eannatum.

"King Destroys Those on his Hit List, One by One – Eannatum:
The First Conqueror." 06 Mar. 2017, https://www.ancient-
origins.net/history/king-destroys-those-his-hit-list-one-one-eannatum-
first-conqueror-part-i-007666.

"Eannatum The Conqueror | Classical Wisdom Weekly." 28 May.
2013,

https://classicalwisdom.com/politics/enemies/eannatum-the-
conqueror/.

"Sumer (Eannatum) - Civilization V Customisation Wiki." 03 Jun.
2016, https://civilization-v-
customisation.fandom.com/wiki/Sumer_(Eannatum).

"Eannatum the Great."
https://sumerianshakespeare.com/37601.html.

"Eannatum - Wikiquote." https://en.wikiquote.org/wiki/Eannatum.

"Eannatum - Bible History." https://bible-
history.com/links/eannatum-2516.

"Stele of the Vultures - Ancient World Magazine." 14 Aug. 2017,

https://www.ancientworldmagazine.com/articles/stele-vultures/.

"Stele of the Vultures - Wikipedia."
https://en.wikipedia.org/wiki/Stele_of_the_Vultures.

"Stele of the Vultures | Ancient monument, Sumer | Britannica."

https://www.britannica.com/place/Stele-of-the-Vultures.

"Sumerian Stele of the Vultures: Oldest Known Historical Records
Carved on Limestone." 01 Sept. 2016,

https://www.ancientpages.com/2016/09/01/sumerian-stele-of-the-vultures-oldest-known-historical-records-carved-on-limestone/.

"Sumerian war chariots deconstructed." 12 Jan. 2012, http://sumerianshakespeare.com/84201.html.

"The Wheels of War: Evolution of the Chariot - History." https://www.historyonthenet.com/the-wheels-of-war-evolution-of-the-chariot.

"Chariot - War Mesopotamian Civilization." https://sites.google.com/site/mesopotamianwarfare/weapon-innovations-in-mesopotamia/sumer/chariot.

"A model of a Sumerian War Chariot." 14 Mar. 2021, http://sumerianshakespeare.com/1273801.html.

"The Wheels of War: Evolution of the Chariot - History." https://www.historyonthenet.com/the-wheels-of-war-evolution-of-the-chariot.

"SUMERIAN TROOPS | Weapons and Warfare." 22 May. 2020, https://weaponsandwarfare.com/2020/05/22/sumerian-troops/.

"Warfare in Sumer - Wikipedia." https://en.wikipedia.org/wiki/Warfare_in_Sumer.

"The Sumerian Military: Professionals of Weaponry and Warfare." 17 Jun. 2016, https://www.ancient-origins.net/history/sumerian-military-professionals-weaponry-and-warfare-006115.

"SUMERIAN TROOPS | Weapons and Warfare." 22 May. 2020, https://weaponsandwarfare.com/2020/05/22/sumerian-troops/.

"Ancient Mesopotamian Warfare | Akkad and Sumer." https://sites.psu.edu/ancientmesopotamianwarfare/.

Chapter 9

"9 Ancient Sumerian Inventions That Changed the World - HISTORY." 01 Aug. 2019,

https://www.history.com/news/sumerians-inventions-mesopotamia.

"Top 10 Sumerian Inventions and Discoveries - Ancient History Lists." 20 Nov. 2019,

https://www.ancienthistorylists.com/mesopotamia-history/top-10-sumerian-inventions-followed-many-civilizations/.

"Razor - Wikipedia." https://en.wikipedia.org/wiki/Razor.

"Who Were the Ancient Sumerians? | Discover Magazine." 10 Nov. 2020,

https://www.discovermagazine.com/planet-earth/who-were-the-ancient-sumerians-and-what-are-they-known-for.

"History of the Sumerians: The 'First' of the Mesopotamians." 06 Dec. 2019,

https://www.realmofhistory.com/2019/12/06/sumerians-first-mesopotamian/.

"What are some of the other things the Sumerians invented?" https://ask.mrdonn.org/meso/43.html.

"The History of Wet Shaving - OriginalShaveCompany.com." 22 Mar. 2016,

https://originalshavecompany.com/the-history-of-wet-shaving/.

Chapter 10

"Sumerian Myths - Grand Valley State University." https://faculty.gvsu.edu/websterm/SumerianMyth.htm.

"Sumerian creation myth - Wikipedia." https://en.wikipedia.org/wiki/Sumerian_creation_myth.

"Sumerian Mythology Index - sacred-texts.com." https://www.sacred-texts.com/ane/sum/.

"Death and Afterlife in Sumerian Beliefs - Ancient Pages." 12 May. 2017,

https://www.ancientpages.com/2017/05/12/death-and-afterlife-in-sumerian-beliefs/.

"What Is Sumerian Mythology? | Only Slightly Biased." https://onlyslightlybiased.com/what-is-sumerian-mythology.

"Sumerian creation myth | Religion Wiki | Fandom."

https://religion.fandom.com/wiki/Sumerian_creation_myth.

"Mesopotamian Creation Myths | Essay | The Metropolitan Museum of Art." https://www.metmuseum.org/toah/hd/epic/hd_epic.htm.

"Eridu Genesis - World History Encyclopedia." 07 May. 2020,

https://www.worldhistory.org/Eridu_Genesis/.

"CREATION MYTHS – AKKADIAN – BABYLONIAN – SUMERIAN - lc5827wdp." 05 Apr.

2013, https://lc5827wdp.wordpress.com/2013/04/05/creation-myths-akkadian-babylonian-sumerian-april-2013/.

"Inanna: A Sneak Peek into the Rebel Ancient Sumerian Goddess."

https://www.timelessmyths.com/mythology/inanna/.

"Sumerian Gods & Goddesses - Transcendence Works!"

https://www.transcendenceworks.com/blog/sumerian-gods-goddesses/.

"'Sumerian Mythology and the Controversy That Surrounds the Anunnaki." 11 Oct. 2020

https://rebirthoftheword.com/sumerian-mythology-and-the-controversy-that-surrounds-the-anunnaki/.

"The origins of human beings according to ancient Sumerian texts." 26 Feb. 2019

https://www.ancient-origins.net/news-human-origins-folklore/origins-human-beings-according-ancient-sumerian-texts-0065

"Ancient Mesopotamian Gods and Goddesses - An/Anu (god)."
http://oracc.museum.upenn.edu/amgg/listofdeities/an/.

"Anu | Mesopotamian god | Britannica."
https://www.britannica.com/topic/Anu.

"Ninhursag - Wikipedia." https://en.wikipedia.org/wiki/Ninhursag.

"Ninhursag - World History Encyclopedia." 26 Jan. 2017,
https://www.worldhistory.org/Ninhursag/.

"Ninhursag | Mesopotamian deity | Britannica."
https://www.britannica.com/topic/Ninhursag.

"Enlil - World History Encyclopedia." 24 Jan. 2017,
https://www.worldhistory.org/Enlil/.

"Enlil - Wikipedia." https://en.wikipedia.org/wiki/Enlil.

"Enlil - Mesopotamian God of Wind and Breath | Mythology.net."
31 Oct. 2016,

https://mythology.net/others/gods/enlil/.

"Ancient Mesopotamian Gods and Goddesses - Enlil/Ellil (god)."
http://oracc.museum.upenn.edu/amgg/listofdeities/enlil/index.html.

"Enki - Wikipedia." https://en.wikipedia.org/wiki/Enki.

"Enki - World History Encyclopedia." 09 Jan. 2017,
https://www.worldhistory.org/Enki/.

"Who was the Sumerian God Enki? | Gaia." 29 Nov. 2019,
https://www.gaia.com/article/who-was-sumerian-god-enki.

"Enki & Enlil - Annunaki." https://www.annunaki.org/enki-enlil/.

"Enki and the world order: translation - University of Oxford."
https://etcsl.orinst.ox.ac.uk/section1/tr113.htm.

"Enki and the World Order (Version 1) - Mesopotamian Gods."
http://www.mesopotamiangods.com/enki-the-world-order-version-
1/.

"Enki and the World Order - Earth-history." https://earth-history.com/Sumer/enki-worldorder.htm.

"Myth, Ritual, and Order in Enki and the World Order."

https://www.academia.edu/14523257/Myth_Ritual_and_Order_in_Enki_and_the_World_Order

Made in United States
Orlando, FL
17 April 2024

45923546R00088